Pieces: Putting Me Back Together

Finding Peace in His Presence

Natasha Janise

Edited by
Nicole Queen

VISION PUBLISHING
HOUSE

Vision Publishing House
support@vision-publishinghouse.com
www.vision-publishinghouse.com

ISBN: 978-1-955297-74-5 (print)
LCCN: 2024925294

This book is established to provide information and inspiration to all readers. It is designed with the understanding that the author is not engaged to render any psychological, legal, or any other kind of professional advice. The content is the sole expression of the author. The author is not liable for any physical, psychological, emotional, financial, or commercial damages, including, but not limited to special, incidental, consequential, or other damages. All readers are responsible for their own choices, actions, and results.

I dedicate this book to my late mother and amazing daughter.

To my beautiful mother: I thank God every day for allowing you to be my mother. I can still feel your warm kisses and sweet embraces. You taught me the true meaning of love. I know you are proud of me, just as I have always been proud of you. I only wish you were here to celebrate this moment with me. You always stood behind me and encouraged me to keep going. I can still remember the excitement in your eyes and voice whenever I shared a new achievement with you. Thank you for helping me become a good mom! All that I am, I learned from you.
This book is dedicated to you, Mom, my first true love.

To my sweet, loving daughter: Oh, how I thank God for sending me an angel. You saved my life! You taught me how to love again. I am so proud of the young lady you have grown up to become. I have learned so much from you. You reminded me to have faith and to trust in the Lord, and I thank you for that. I thank you for your unconditional love. I will forever have your back, no matter what. If you need a blocker, I will guard your front, as well. You will always be the love of my life!

With all of my love,
Your daughter and mother

"Even though I walk through the valley of the shadow of death, I will fear no evil, for you are with me; your rod and your staff, they comfort me"

— Psalm 23:4 (ESV)

Contents

Introduction

One of the reasons I decided to sit down and pour my heart out on paper was because I chose to live again. I reached a point in my life where I felt tired of not feeling fulfilled. I was tired of being tired, and I simply wanted to live again. As a child, I always loved writing and would pretend I was an author working on a book. I would start to journal events, but then either misplace the book or not complete it at all.

Beyond my desire to live again, a prophet once approached me and said, "God said to write the book." At that point, I didn't know what book God was referring to, but as I completed my grief therapy sessions, it hit me—that book. The thought of writing a book about the people I loved and lost brought tears that came streaming down my face. It was time for me to sit down and be obedient to God. I thought back to the beginning of the storm, realizing I was still standing in the midst of it, even as I wrote this book.

I began to reflect on the early days of the storm when it was just wild winds. As the clouds darkened and the storm rolled in, I inadvertently changed course, leading me into the longest storm of my life. The storm of grief escalated to a catastrophic level 5, and I was exhausted from being battered by the uncontrollable waves and undercurrents. I

Introduction

couldn't understand why this storm seemed endless or why I couldn't control the ship—my life—and navigate out of it.

It wasn't until I realized that I wasn't the captain of this ship—God was. He wanted me to have faith and surrender the reins to Him. When I released "control" and gave God my YES, that was the pivotal moment that set me on a course of healing. I decided that the only way for me to truly heal was to write down some of the major moments of my life. I invite you to join me as I share my testimonies, tears, and joy through stories of grief and healing, love and laughter. Please come on this journey with an open heart and mind, asking God to help you receive any message meant for you.

Chapter 1: You Knew Me

"Before I formed you in the womb I knew you, before you were born I set you apart; I appointed you as a prophet to the nations."

— Jeremiah 1:5 (NIV)

* * *

"You knew me since you were a little girl." Tears streamed down my face, breaking free like a dam that had finally burst. Something about the prophet's words triggered a flood of memories. Memories surfaced from when I was about four or five years old—memories of God speaking to me. I knew God from a young age.

He was my friend, my protector, and my father. The prophet continued, "I held you in my arms and protected you from so many things. You knew who I was," said the spirit of the Lord. How could I forget? Why would I forget? It had been so long, and what I had taken for silence after I last spoke to God made me assume He wasn't there. After receiving that message, memories of me talking to God and Him speaking to me flooded back. I hadn't understood or realized then that my Father had always been with me.

1

That weekend, I went to a spiritual conference. It was my first time attending an event such as this. The room was layered with a mixture of prophetic voices and spirit-filled tears, as the faint scent of anointing oil lingered in the air. The warmth of raised hands during prayer grounded me, even as my heart raced with anticipation. A friend had invited me, and now I know it was by design—God moved through her to ask me. As the prophet spoke, his words reverberated through me, not just as sound, but as a force. I felt free. I experienced a sudden warmth in my chest, spreading outwards until my entire body seemed to be filled with an inexplicable force. It was as if God Himself was reaching out to remind me of who I was. So many things changed in my life that weekend. When I arrived home, I sat down and exhaled. The quiet hum of the house surrounded me, contrasting the power-packed service I had just left behind. It felt like I was releasing all the pent-up emotions that had raged through my body for so long. I felt a difference in my spirit. I felt a shift!

To give you a glimpse of my childhood, let me take you back for a moment. Growing up, my mother made sure we were loved, well-fed, and clean as a whistle. My parents separated when I was about two, but it didn't matter much because we lived in a two-family house in New York. My grandparents, along with my uncles and aunt, lived upstairs. As you can imagine, we had a blast. There was so much love, and I thank God for that. Hallelujah, glory—I thank God for that.

My mother always ensured our hair was neatly combed with beautiful bows, and our clothes were always clean and pressed. Somehow, our shoes always matched our outfits. The primary color I loved was pink, while my sister wore purple. My brother was dressed like a miniature gentleman, complete with a suit for church and sharp, polished shoes. Every Sunday, my mother made sure we attended church, even when she had to work. On those days, my grandmother would step in and take us. Back then, it truly took a village to raise a family. Our neighbor and family friend drove us to church each week since my grandmother didn't have a driver's license.

We children had to sit in the front row at church, which I absolutely dreaded. The hard wooden benches seemed to press against my back, and the faint scent of old hymnals and polished pews filled the air.

Without fail, I would fall asleep during the pastor's sermon. "Keep your eyes open," I would tell myself. "What is wrong with you?" No amount of self-coaching helped; I was out like a light every time. Whenever I briefly woke up, I would glance up and see my godmother in the choir, also dozing. We must have had some rough nights before!

After the service, the children would go downstairs for Sunday school. Sometimes, I would beg my grandmother to let me go home with her instead, and once in a while, she would agree. I loved stopping by our neighbor's house for a cup of tea and some bakery cookies. That was the highlight of my Sundays. On those days, when my mother asked what I learned in Sunday school, I would repeat the question to stall. "Sunday school? What did I learn in Sunday school today?" My sister would shout, "*Nothing*, because she didn't go!" Oh, how I wanted to tape that cute little bow over her mouth. "Natasha," my mother would yell. "Did you come home, drink tea, and eat pastries with Nana?" I repeated, "Come home? Eat pastries?" There I went with the questions, again. "Girl, don't play with me. I will beat your butt!" my mother yelled. I quickly responded. "Yes, Mommy, I did."

Sunday school bored me. The Bible's language was foreign to me, and I felt lost at every turn of the stories. And when I learned that Jesus was God, and God was also the Holy Spirit, I couldn't understand how one being could be the Father, the Son, and the Holy Spirit at the same time. When I brought this up to my mother, she explained different Bible stories to me. I began to understand more, but not with the clarity I have now.

Even now, as I write this book, memories resurface, taking me on a journey through time. Don't worry, readers, I'll guide you through every step. That night, after I returned home from the conference, I reflected on the words I had received: "You knew who I was as a child." I did. I recalled moments when I simply knew things, but couldn't explain how.

One Saturday, my family traveled to Westchester for a celebration at my great-aunt's building. The party was held in the community center on the first floor. We had so much fun. As a child, I was meticulous about what I ate, who made it, and how clean the area was. I must have been four or five when I had my first clear encounter with God. I needed to use the bathroom but didn't want to use the community one, so I begged my mother to take me upstairs to my great-aunt's apartment. My great-aunt, my grandmother's sister, kept her home spotless, just like my grandmother and mother.

We turned right down the hallway after entering the apartment, with the bathroom straight ahead. My great-aunt and great-uncle's bedroom was on the left. I halted at the doorway, unable to move. My mother leaned in and whispered, "Come on, Natasha. He's asleep." I looked up at her and said, "No, Mommy, he's dying. He's dead." She pressed her hand on my back and guided me into the bathroom. "Don't say that; he's just sleeping," she said. "No, Mommy, he is dying," I insisted. She sighed and told me to hurry up.

The party carried on, full of laughter and chatter. When it ended, we said our goodbyes and drove home, exhaustion settling over us. We changed into our pajamas, said our prayers, and my mother turned out the light. Moments after she left our room, I heard the phone ring. I sat up, straining to listen. I heard my mother gasp, "Oh no!" followed by a heavy sigh.

She returned to our room. "Natasha, why did you say Uncle died?" she asked. "Because he was," I replied. "But how did you know?" she pressed. "I don't know. I think God told me," I said. "OK, go to sleep," she whispered. The next day, I learned that my great-uncle had passed away that night. My great-aunt went upstairs, expecting to find him peacefully asleep, only to discover that wasn't the case. Looking back, I understand now that those moments were God's way of showing me that His presence was never far, even in the midst of uncertainty and fear.

As a child, I didn't understand the magnitude of my words that night. Reflecting back on it now sends chills down my spine because I didn't understand the gift that I had over my life. I didn't understand it back then, but now I know that it was God.

Chapter 2: God Knows

"God is our refuge and strength, an ever-present help in trouble."

— Psalm 46:1 (NIV)

* * *

Running around and playing were the first and last things on my mind as a child. We would run outside carefree, feeling the warm sun on our backs and the cool breeze rustling through the leaves, with the weight of nothing on our shoulders. We went to church every Sunday, blessed our dinner, prayed before going to sleep, and thanked God for allowing us to wake up in the morning.

Well, if I'm being honest, if we started the morning acting up, my mother would say, "Did you thank God for allowing you to wake up?" As quickly as I could, I would silently say in my head, "Thank you, Father, for allowing me to wake up. Amen." Then I would respond, "Yes, I did, thank God." My mother would raise an eyebrow and reply, "When... just now?" Of course, I would answer with, "When?" I could feel my mother's eyes piercing my soul. She couldn't stand it when I responded to a question with a question.

I was always a respectful child because I knew how hard my mother worked. She had one golden rule: Never let our school call her to say we weren't listening. She always told us, "Don't you embarrass me, and have people think you don't know any better."

My family followed the motto, It takes a village to raise a child. If I got in trouble for playing rough outside or not listening in the house, the telephone would ring, and I would stop. Next thing you know, if my brother or sister answered the phone, they would say, "Pop-Pop said to come upstairs." My brother would start to laugh, and I'd fall out on the floor, ready to die. I couldn't believe someone had told on me. "Where is the loyalty?" I would think to myself, with the new realization that in this house, honesty trumped sibling alliances. So, not only did I have fear and respect for God, but I also had fear and respect for my mother and grandfather, whose stern looks and words carried the weight of generations of lessons.

I remember one day, maybe in second or third grade, we got off the yellow school bus outside the front of our elementary school. Some of the kids would run to the back and play unsupervised. You already know, I followed the rules and wasn't down for it. One of the girls asked if I was coming, and I said, "No." She asked why not. I didn't feel like going into detail about it.

So, I just started walking toward the school. A few of the kids ran up to me and said, "Your mother won't find out; she's not here." I replied, "But God is." The kids just looked at me and ran off, their laughter fading into the distance. I stood there for a moment, feeling a quiet assurance that even if they didn't understand, I wasn't alone. I took a deep breath, turned my back on the fading commotion, stepped inside the school, and started my day. Even though I hadn't spoken to God, I could still feel His presence. I couldn't figure out where He was, but I knew He was there. It wasn't until years later, as life's challenges tested me in ways I couldn't have imagined, that I truly understood: the spirit of the Lord had always been within me, guiding and holding me steady.

Chapter 3: Footprints

* * *

As a child, I went to the beach every Sunday in the summer. A few times, my mother went with us, but she usually had to work on the weekends and missed out on the whole beach experience. Back in the day, the entire neighborhood helped raise your kids, so we would go to the beach with our friend and her mother, who were our neighbors.

On Saturday nights, I would always get excited, packing my bag with everything I might need. Baby oil was for my tanning, and of course, I had to sneak that into the bag. Growing up as an African American girl, we were told to use sunscreen, and sometimes I did apply SPF 90, but then I'd go to the other extreme and apply baby oil so my skin could glisten in the sunlight.

The only thing I did not like about going to the beach was that we were a little low on funds. My mother would always make peanut butter and jelly sandwiches, which drove me crazy—absolutely crazy! I could never tell if I was crunching on the nuts or sand. If you have ever been to the beach, you know that sand gets everywhere, and I mean everywhere.

Going to the beach was peaceful. I felt at one with nature and life. We went to the beach every summer from when I was in the fourth grade until the seventh grade. We would lay out on the sand for a while, then run down to the water and splash around. The warm sand slipped through my fingers, and the rhythmic crashing of the waves created a soothing background, as we built sandcastles and dug holes to put our feet in. Sometimes, we dug the holes so deep we struck water at the bottom. I used to wish it was gold so we could buy turkey and cheese sandwiches instead of eating peanut butter and jelly sandwiches on the beach. Boy, oh boy, I used to get so upset eating that sandwich, crunching and not knowing if it was a peanut or sand.

On this particular day, we went out to the water, and the tide kept pulling further out. We kept walking out since the water was so low that we didn't even realize how far we had gone. Suddenly, the waves started coming in hard, one after another. Normally, we would jump right over them and ride them back in, but it didn't happen that way that day.

I should mention one crucial detail: I didn't know how to swim. I tried to jump as high as my short legs would allow, but because the waves were coming in so fast, I jumped right into a breaking wave. It slammed my head into the bottom of the seafloor, nearly knocking me unconscious. All I felt was pain and confusion. Strangely enough, I felt at peace; I wasn't scared. I couldn't open my eyes because the water burned so badly. At that point, I decided to just lie there. Somehow, another wave came and brought me back to shore. I stood up, choking on water, while my sister and friend laughed nervously. They started screaming, "Oh my goodness, that wave was crazy!" I said, "Yeah, that wave almost killed me." As I stood on the shore, still coughing and trembling, a strange calm settled over me, as though an unseen hand had placed me back on safe ground. I knew, even then, that it wasn't just chance—it was something more. That event didn't stop me from wanting to enjoy the water; it just made me more aware and cautious about what I did.

Little did I know, that wouldn't be my last encounter with a near-death experience. The following year, my family went upstate to my mother's best friend's house. I loved going there. It was a peaceful environment, with no one for miles along the route. My mother's friend and her husband owned a lot of land, and her husband would build another section of the house each year.

That year, my mother's friend said, "Hey, let's go over one town to my friend's house; we can get in the pool there." So we went, and all the kids got in the pool. The lady warned us to be careful because the pool dropped deep in the middle, about eight feet. My mother said, "Oh no, Natasha can't swim." The woman laughed and said I had better stay toward the edge of the pool. So I did—or at least I thought I did. To take you back a second, I never told my friend's mother that I almost drowned that day at the beach because I knew they wouldn't let us go back in the water. I also never told my mother because she wouldn't allow us to go back to the beach.

We were excited to get into this pool. My brother and the boys who knew how to swim were in the front playing basketball. I started walking around inside the pool, while my sister jumped up and down in the water. She knew how to swim, but I didn't. I went around one full lap while holding onto the side because, for some reason, the floor of the pool was slippery. I let go of the side, and suddenly, I slipped and drifted out to the middle of the pool.

All I remembered was coming up for air and going under again. I was told my mother was screaming, "Oh my God, somebody help her." My mother's friends later told me that she started to jump in, but the woman grabbed her and said, "Carol, you don't know how to swim." My mother also started yelling for my sister to grab me. I remember trying to reach my sister, but she pushed the water away from her and toward me. In hindsight, I realize that if I had panicked, I could have drowned her too. Somehow, no one could explain it, but as quickly as I had slipped out to the middle of the pool, I returned to the edge. The moment my hand gripped the pool's edge, relief and disbelief surged through me. *How did I make it back here?* I remembered seeing a light and feeling confusion, just like during the incident at the beach.

I climbed out from the side, and my mother hugged me tightly. She said, "Oh my God, how did you make it to the side?" I said, "I don't know." I was shaking and so scared inside—I really thought I was going to die. "How did I get to the side?" I asked myself. Deep down, I knew it was God. I knew it wasn't my time. I knew, just like before, He placed me on dry land. I knew He was with me the entire time. My mother asked me over and over, "Are you alright?" I replied, "Yes" each time. I couldn't tell her I was shaking in my swimsuit. She would never forgive herself for listening to me and allowing me to enter the pool.

I knew my mother was distressed enough. I didn't want to add to her worry. So, I asked if I could use the bathroom. They showed me where it was. My mother asked if I wanted her to go with me, but I told her no. Once I entered the bathroom, I immediately fell to the floor, crying. I said, "Thank you, Father, for sparing my life. Thank you, God, for not letting me die and taking me away from my mom." I was more upset about how my mother would feel without me than the fact that I almost drowned again.

I stood up, wiped my tears, and went back outside. My mother was walking toward me, coming to check if I was alright. I said yes and asked to get back in the water. She said, "Absolutely not!" Her friends shouted, "Let the girl get in the water!" They clearly weren't thinking straight. I reassured my mother that I would just sit on the edge with my feet in the water. She asked, "Why?" I said, "If I don't, I'll be afraid to ever go into the water again." I held on tight, slid in, and got back out. My mother said she was so proud of me. I rested that night in her arms.

That evening, I had nightmares of drowning, but I didn't share that with anyone. When I jumped up from one of the dreams and lay back down, I felt a sense of peace wash over me and my life. I started making a connection to how I felt as a little girl when I sensed God's presence. It was God who carried me to safety, one set of footprints. I knew that the water encounter was one with God. As I lay in bed that night, the memory of the water and the inexplicable peace I felt reminded me that, even in my most helpless moments, I was never truly alone.

Chapter 4: Memories

* * *

That night, I continued to reflect on what the prophetess shared with me: God said, "I never left you. I was with you the whole time." Over and over, I replayed those words while thinking back to significant events in my life, and another memory came to mind. I was in high school, and it was always my sister and my best friend. We walked everywhere together.

During that time, there were a lot of teen events and day parties, which were absolutely the best! There was one party in particular that stood out to me. This party wasn't at our regular lounge area. That lounge was safe and provided us the space to dance and enjoy ourselves. But this one night, we went to a different lounge, which gave me a dark feeling right from the start. A wave of nausea rolled through me, like a warning bell tolling deep inside. It wasn't just the usual flutter of nerves;

it was a gnawing, insistent dread that twisted my gut. I always wrote it off as me just being nervous around new people. Not this time! I felt sick but didn't listen to the feeling.

We went inside. The music was good, but the place seemed small—extremely small. I automatically looked around for exits and didn't see any. It was at that moment I said, "I think we should leave." We were standing on the main level of the lounge, toward the middle, closer to a door that led downstairs.

We went down where there was more music and some people we knew. I still felt like we should leave. I looked around, and I could see no exits down there. We started heading back up the stairs, and I was in front. Once we reached the main level again, I suddenly froze, and my gut told me to turn around. I saw two guys arguing in front of us, and I knew that wasn't good. A sick feeling came over me, and I knew to immediately turn back around and head to the basement stairs. As soon as we neared the bottom of the stairs, people started flying down over our heads, screaming, "They are shooting."

We ran together behind a chair and dropped to the floor. Next thing I knew, a boy grabbed my friend and tried to put her in front of him. She went off on him, and we jumped up, and he let her go. All the while, the DJ still played music. The police showed up and had to tell the DJ to turn the music off. It was safe to leave.

We walked home that night, and I thanked God all the way. It was crazy because that night, I didn't have any nightmares. That "gut feeling" I had—I knew it was God who told us to go back and protected us. In that moment, I marveled at how often I ignored those subtle nudges, not fully understanding they were divine whispers. It was as though God had been tapping on my shoulder all along, protecting me even when I strayed.

Throughout my life, there have been many events, both good and bad. Nonetheless, God was there for both. His hand was over me the entire time. These events helped shape me into who I would become. While God's hands were on my life, the enemy still tried to sneak in and plant seeds that could cause structural damage later on in life. Like a careful gardener, God was nurturing me, but weeds of fear and trauma tried to take root, threatening to choke out the growth He intended.

Pieces: Putting Me Back Together

Another traumatic event occurred during high school. In high school, we had the option to take additional classes at night school and summer school. I took two classes in summer school my junior year so that when my senior year came, I would only have a half-day of classes and could relax. Little did I know, this would come at the expense of my peace.

One summer day, a loud commotion occurred as I sat in music class, bored out of my mind and exhausted from the heat trapped inside that room. Our class was at the end of the hallway, so if you were walking down the hall, you could walk straight into the class. My summer music teacher kept the door open to allow the hot air to flow out of the room.

While I sat at my desk, I turned to see a group of boys chasing another boy into our room. The boy, clearly scared, ran behind the teacher, grabbing onto him. He then unknowingly ran into a closet.

All of a sudden, the group of boys ran out, and the boy stumbled out, collapsing with blood and muscle hanging from his face. I'll never forget the blood that splattered onto my desk. I had nightmares for weeks but never told my mother. I didn't want to worry her or put any additional stress on her.

Months later, I finally told her what had happened. As a teen, I didn't know what I know now. That event was traumatic and caused post-traumatic symptoms to surface. It took years of silence before I could admit that my avoidance wasn't strength—it was denial. Only when I began my grief recovery did I realize that God was inviting me to acknowledge my wounds and let Him heal them. Eventually, I suppressed my feelings and memories. It wasn't until my grief recovery in later years that I realized how all of these events had affected me.

After these events, there was a period where I only spoke to God to say grace, bless the food, and pray at night. Toward the end of my senior year of high school, I drifted away from God. I still obeyed Him because that was instilled in me, but that was the extent of it. Obedience was familiar– almost automatic– but intimacy with God was foreign. I didn't know that faith was more than routine—it was a relationship built on trust and conversation. I'm not sure why I drifted away. Maybe I wanted to be so grown up and busy with life that I ultimately left out the most essential part of my life—God.

Having a relationship with God was more of a conflict for me. I thought that if you were in God's presence you had to be perfect. No mistakes! No fun! I thought it had to be all or nothing. I know I didn't want to be a hypocrite and praise God, then turn around and live an ungodly life. I said to myself, "Self, you are far from perfect and that is not what God wants." I had this entire image in my head that every strand of hair had to be perfectly slicked back, my clothing had to be free of wrinkles, and I needed to sit up straight, cross my feet at the ankles, and fold my hands—believing that was the only way God would accept me.

I knew I was far from that. I was respectful, yet adventurous. I was kind, but could cut you up with my tongue. I was observant and somewhat of an introvert with extrovert qualities. I felt that this just didn't fit the mold. I didn't want to disappoint my Heavenly Father. I didn't grasp at that age that God knew me. There are so many billions of people in the world, and I never considered that God truly knew me. As a teenager, it wasn't clear to me that God is omniscient. He has perfect knowledge of all things.

One vital lesson that all children, especially teens should learn is the Word. Reading the Bible helps to gain a better understanding of God's Word, and build an intimate relationship with Him. The Bible says that God is all-knowing.

"You have searched me, Lord, and you know me. You know when I sit and when I rise; you perceive my thoughts from afar."

— Psalms 139: 1-2

I truly believe that guiding an individual to Psalms 1-16 would help them gain a better understanding of how well God knows them. If only I had known the importance of reading and understanding the Word and realized that God would have accepted me for who I was, my teenage years would have been much different!

Despite this, faith was always a part of my upbringing. As I previously mentioned, we always attended church throughout our childhood years. We were involved in everything from the youth choir to teaching primary Sunday school. We gave the little ones Bible coloring pages with images of Jesus and the cross. I believe this is what helped me feel grounded. I knew God was there, but I didn't know how to have a relationship with Him. Now, looking back, I see that God was patiently waiting, ready to teach me that His presence wasn't just in the moments of crisis, but in every breath and heartbeat, longing for me to draw near.

Chapter 5: Seeds

"There is a time for everything, and a season for every activity under the heavens."

— Ecclesiastes 3:1 (NIV)

* * *

I was a great daughter, never giving my mother any problems because I feared God, my mother, and my grandfather. The fear was more about not wanting to disappoint them. Toward the end of my high school junior year, one of my uncles drove my mother and me upstate New York to visit a college, and boy, was it in the backwoods. There was no way I was attending that school. The hate for us Black folks was undeniable. You could see it in the looks on people's faces, and the feeling in my stomach confirmed it. The glares were sharp, almost tangible, piercing through the humid summer air. The knot in my stomach twisted tighter with each step we took, a silent alarm that echoed the unspoken hostility around us.

Due to my mother's hectic work schedule, there was no way she could drive me down to tour my other option in Virginia. So, I accepted an offer at an HBCU in Virginia. Now, I don't know why I did that, considering my brother, who is six years older than me, went to a different HBCU in Virginia, and I thought that was the longest ride of my life! My thoughts then and now: Why would this be a good idea? Oh, I know why—my friends also accepted offers there. I went off the information my friends brought back from their visit to the school and decided to attend.

The time came for me to go away to college. We packed the car, and my mother drove me down with all my belongings. My sister and best friend came along for the ride. We pulled up to the school from the back, and boy, oh boy. Well, needless to say, that was a double negative for me. I wasn't getting out of the car. The buildings near the school were burnt down and abandoned.

My friends decided to attend the summer program for freshmen, and warned me to stay away because the college had started enforcing strict rules. After calling home to my grandfather and letting him speak to my mother, we headed back home with the same packed car and an angry mother, sister, and friend. They had to endure the ride back with the same items piled on their heads and laps. To make matters worse, before we returned home, my mother drove further south to North Carolina to visit our family, then drove back to New York.

What I didn't know was how that semester off would affect my life. Every morning, I would walk upstairs in our two-family house to sit with my grandparents. By this point, my grandfather was in a wheel-chair due to back injuries and surgery. My cousin, an older woman who was my mother's first cousin, would come over, too. Her presence brought me so much joy! Even as I type this now, memories of our time together peacefully pop into my head.

She used to come with us to the beach when we were young. I'll never forget one time when she walked into the water, which was a little below her knees. Suddenly, the tide pulled the water out, causing the sand to slowly disappear from under her feet, and a wave hit her hard, knocking her to her knees. She started screaming, "Help, I'm drown-ing!" while on her hands and knees. Our neighbor, my friend's mother, called out her name and said, "Stand up." We laughed and laughed. She stood up, wiped her face, and said, "Oh, I thought I was drowning." I loved her so much.

One day, I was upstairs, and she asked if I could braid her hair. I said sure. I combed and oiled her scalp, and she relaxed with a smile, saying thank you. She always told me she loved my smile—it brought her peace. Little did she know, her presence brought me peace. One week, she didn't come over. My grandmother asked if I could go next door to her house, and help her wash her hair. I agreed. When I walked in, she looked different. I smiled and asked her how she was doing, and she smiled back and thanked me for coming.

As I started to take the cornrows out of her hair, I realized that the hair wasn't attached. Every braid I unloosened came out in my hand. Each braid that slipped from her scalp felt like a thread unraveling from the fabric of my childhood memories, leaving behind the stark reality of loss. I wanted to throw up, cry, and faint all at once. So many emotions flooded my heart, but I knew I had to hold it together.

Back then, Black families tended to keep everything private—everything was a secret. I realized something was medically wrong, that she likely had cancer or another illness. My hand must have fallen on her head because she asked if I was okay. I took a deep breath and said, "Yes, I'm okay. Your hair is so soft. You look beautiful without it. You are so beautiful." She smiled and closed her eyes while I massaged her head.

When I was done, I went home, and collapsed onto the cold tiles of the bathroom floor, as if the ground itself could absorb the weight of my sorrow. My mother knocked on the door and asked what happened. I told her, and she was angry with my grandmother for not telling me beforehand. My grandmother apologized, not realizing her hair would fall out so quickly. My cousin later called to speak with my mother, likely to check on how I was doing. I whispered to my mother to tell her I was okay. A few months later, she passed away.

I felt sad and angry at the same time, but I never connected those emotions to God. It was like I had abandoned Him without even knowing it. My anger wasn't directed at God; it was directed at the world. Why did she have to die? I could only imagine what her young son was going through. I didn't know what to say or do to ease his pain, so, unfortunately, I said nothing. I held everything inside and carried on with life.

A few months later, I was set to go to college, but that separation anxiety kicked in, and I was afraid to leave my mother. I didn't want to end up like my little cousin—without a mother. From about ages 3 to 9, I had felt an anxiety that took over my body every time my mother had to leave. I always felt the need to protect her and be close. Looking back, I know that feeling manifested from losing family members. Growing up and witnessing the deaths of family members made me anticipate losing my mother. That feeling began to resurface for a moment.

This time, I left because one of my close friends was already at this college. Before enrolling, I had visited her for homecoming two years in a row. For the life of me, I don't know why I didn't pick this college first. My best friend also enrolled with me, which eased my anxiety a bit. My mother reassured me she was healthy and would be alright.

During my gap year, I had a boyfriend whom I met in middle school —6th grade, to be exact. I knew he liked me, and I liked him, but I was shy, innocent, and young. His mother eventually enrolled him in a Catholic middle and high school to keep him safe and away from the local kids who hung around getting into trouble.

We ran into each other in the neighborhood during my senior year of high school. We dated from about May of my senior year until that August when I initially thought I was going away to school. We were both upset when I planned to leave for Virginia. When I returned home after a week and took my gap year, we were both excited. But reality set in when it was time for me to leave again. This time, it was for good. We talked on the phone every day, which helped with my homesickness.

Over time, it became too difficult for me to commute home often to see him, and it strained our relationship. I allowed an older, hurt person to project her pain onto me by telling me he would probably cheat on me. She said, "You better not come home just to see him. That's what they do, cheat!" It's strange how one comment, seemingly innocuous, can grow roots so deep that they crack the foundation of trust you thought was unbreakable. That seed was planted in my mind, and I began to doubt. Looking back, I realize how easy it was for the enemy to use others' words to sow doubt. It's in these whispers of insecurity that

God's voice can seem the quietest, overshadowed by the loud clamor of fear and uncertainty. I didn't realize then that the enemy often uses people to plant seeds of doubt in our minds, knowing we'll water them ourselves. I stopped going home as much, and one day, a freshman guy on campus stopped me and asked my name and which dorm I stayed in. Long story short, we started talking, and the guilt was immediate. I told my boyfriend right away.

He was crushed, and so was I. Other events happened that hurt him further. Losing that relationship was a significant loss for me. I never wanted to hurt him. We continued to talk periodically, but it was never the same. He started seeing someone else, and the rest is history. I held on to the "what-if" for years, wondering if we still had a chance, but life had different plans.

My college relationship was one I would later regret. Don't get me wrong; I enjoyed the time with my college boyfriend, and we shared many memories, but there was always that "what if" scenario I allowed to replay in my head.

I didn't realize that grief played a role in many of my relationships. Grief, subtle yet relentless, wove itself into my heart, shaping how I saw love and commitment. It whispered that love was fleeting and that loss was inevitable, creating a barrier to trust. It played a significant part in my relationship with my older cousin who passed away and with my first love, which ended. Both caused grief. Many people don't realize that grief is defined as "the natural reaction to loss." The Mayo Clinic states that grief is both a universal and personal experience.

Individual experiences of grief vary and are influenced by the nature of the loss. Some examples of loss include the death of a loved one, the ending of a meaningful relationship, job loss, or the loss of independence due to a disability, as stated by many grief experts. While you cannot, and should not, compare the two losses, they were significant in their own ways.

Granted, there were things in my relationship with my ex that we both could have done differently. If it was meant to be, it would have been. I learned during this journey called life that God allows certain people to come into your life for different reasons and seasons. I learned to cherish the people in my life. During this break up, I lost a really good friend. It was only later, after losing other people I loved, that I understood each relationship held a lesson—a preparation for the future losses that life would inevitably bring.

After editing this book and reflecting on everything, I wondered why it was so easy for me to believe and embrace the seed of doubt planted in my mind. I think it's because I saw the adult relationships around me fail, and I thought mine would, too. Although my childhood sweetheart treated me with kindness, respect, and unconditional love, I must have felt like it would end eventually. So, why get hurt? Instead, I hurt him and, ultimately, myself in the process. We still care for each other to this day, and I thank God for allowing me to share that season with him. Some seeds are planted to teach, others to challenge, but all are part of the garden that shapes who we become. I now know that with God's guidance, even the seeds sown in doubt can be uprooted, making space for new growth.

While these seeds were planted at that moment, the roots left lasting effects which would cascade causing a ripple effect throughout my life. I unknowingly continued to water the seed of doubt, which then split and rooted out to mistrust. It wasn't only that seed that caused this. It was the lack of the Word.

The message of the seed in the Bible is two-fold. In Matthew 13, one parable spoken by Jesus is "The Parable of the Sower." This message speaks about seeds that were sown and where they landed. Jesus explains the reason for the parable in the bible saying, "He replied, because the knowledge of the secrets of the kingdom of heaven has been given to you, but not them. Whoever has will be given more, and they will have an abundance. Whoever does not have, even what they have will be taken from them" (Matthew 13:11-12). While I knew of the Lord, I lacked knowledge. So, the bad seed planted turned into weeds, which overgrew the garden, similar to the story in the Bible, which suggests that the good seeds were taken away. The Word of God states:

"My people are destroyed from lack of knowledge."

— Hosea 4:6 (NIV)

When you lack knowledge, it becomes easy for the enemy to plant seeds. Yes, the bad seeds were planted, but like "The Parable of the Sower," both the good and bad seeds grew together, but God allowed the weeds to be pulled and burned during harvest season. This is my harvest season! God pulled and burned the weeds because He loves me.

Chapter 6: Trials

"The righteous cry out, and the Lord hears them; he delivers them from all their troubles. The Lord is close to the brokenhearted and saves those who are crushed in spirit."

— Psalm 34:17-18 (NIV)

* * *

My college years were amazing– filled with excitement, late-night study sessions, friendships forged over shared laughter, and the occasional dance party that lifted our spirits. Those were the days when the world felt wide open, with endless possibilities waiting just around the corner. Most of you know the saying, *"All good things must come to an end."* It was time to live the life I had prepared for. After graduating from college, I started my career working in Delaware. Six months later, I decided to move back home to New York. While I enjoyed Delaware's peace, I wasn't satisfied with the pay. Moving back home felt both comforting and uncertain, like stepping into familiar waters with the tide subtly shifting beneath my feet.

Before leaving my little studio in Delaware, I reflected on life, future goals, and expectations. I had it all planned out. There wasn't anything anyone could tell me. My plan was to continue with my career, buy a house, get a dog to love, and, last but not least, find a man to complete my already planned fairy tale wedding. Yes, that's right! All I needed to do was pick him up and place him where he needed to be. And I was serious about that. The crazy thing is, if you caught me on a different day, I would have been perfectly fine with not getting married because I had started to love my peace.

I was happy alone, with no expectations, no feelings getting involved, and no one getting hurt—life was good! Little did I know that this would be the decade of huge shifts in my life.

It was summer when I returned home and immediately secured a job. My friends and I always enjoyed the summer months in NYC. We partied on boat rides, at clubs, at private parties at Chelsea Piers, and more. Summers were everything! One weekend, Labor Day weekend, we went to a Caribbean club in New Rochelle called The Carib. That was an amazing place to party, with great vibes and guaranteed amazing music.

One night, we went to The Carib to enjoy ourselves- which is where I met my daughter's father. We bonded and had a relationship that lasted a few years. I was hesitant to date him because I didn't feel like forming emotional bonds with anyone, but eventually, I did. I also felt like I was forcing the relationship just to get over whatever slump I was in. Everyone kept telling me, *"You have to get out there and date."* Now, I know that if you aren't healed from what you went through, you're doomed to repeat the same circumstances, adding to your baggage.

At this point in my life, I still wasn't in a place where I had constant communication with God, and I didn't know Him at the level I do now. I felt as though God was a distant figure, watching but not intervening. In hindsight, I realize He was waiting for me to invite Him into my chaos, to recognize His subtle presence amid my noisy life.

As time went on in this relationship, we decided to go our separate ways. That's when I found out I was expecting. This was a blow because I felt like my plan had collapsed. Everything was going differently than planned, except for me securing a job. I didn't realize that everything was actually coming together the way God intended it to be.

People were judgmental and said, *"You're not supposed to have a baby out of wedlock"* and *"Children of unwed couples are mistakes."* While God wants us to be married, He never makes mistakes. One thing for sure and two things for certain, God doesn't make mistakes! God knew my baby girl before she was even in my womb. So, the children many people speak negatively about are God's children. He is their Father, Protector, and Provider. It is said that God chooses everyone for a purpose.

While I asked God to forgive me for not being married, I never felt guilty for carrying His child. It was during this time that I started talking to God more and growing closer in the spiritual realm. People tried to pass judgment, but God made me so that judgment never bothered me. I always felt that it was that person's problem to deal with, not mine. I was good!

I prayed over my baby every night, talked to her, read books, and played mellow music for her. I knew in my spirit that this baby would be someone special. As time passed, the support and happiness of a new baby in our family grew. Months went by, and I had my little angel. I looked at her and felt a sense of peace as if I were holding my very own angel. I prayed over her life every day.

She was born in April, and in August, after many months of my grandfather being in the hospital, he passed away. When I received the news, I wrapped my baby up and ran to the hospital, holding her tight while breaking down in tears. I told the nurse I just wanted my baby to see her grandfather, who was really her great-grandfather. It was too late. He was gone.

My grandfather had been sick, and it wasn't safe for my daughter to be around him since she had just been born. All I could do was take a picture of her and have my grandmother tape it to the wall in his hospital room. I remember my grandmother saying,

"Your grandfather doesn't speak when we are in there with him, but the nurse told me she was in his room, and the picture fell off the wall. He lifted his head and told the nurse to pick his baby up." That brought tears to my eyes. I wasn't sure if he understood what was happening around

him. I know my daughter would have loved him, and he would have loved her if time had allowed them to be together.

What I'm about to share is my truth. It's not meant to hurt anyone, but it is what it is. My mother and father dated in high school, married for several years, and separated when I was two. Whatever their reasons, they were between them. Sometimes people need healing from previous life events, and separating is best. Staying together can sometimes cause more damage than good.

I never thought much about my father not being there because we lived in a house filled with love and people. When my mother was growing up, life was difficult because my grandmother and grandfather both had healing to do, so they went through some struggles. As my siblings and I grew up, our grandparents were pretty much in the healing process, and life was better for us. My grandfather was, in my eyes, my father. He loved, protected, and helped provide when needed.

My grandfather would always call me to hand him a wrench or whatever tool he needed while fixing something. I remember praying, *"Lord, please let me know what he asked for."* My grandfather would say, *"Pass me the wrench."* I would look at the whole toolbox filled with hundreds of tools and stand there, puzzled.

One of the first times he asked, I tried to lift the heavy box to bring all the tools. Now, I was always this tiny, petite thing. My grandfather sat up and yelled, *"Girl, are you crazy? You're going to hurt yourself."* He took the box and said, *"Now sit down and let me teach you some things."* After that moment, my grandfather would call me to help whenever he worked in our apartment. I felt so proud to be able to help him.

I loved my grandfather and was crushed when he passed away. I never had any regrets when it came to him. When I was younger, I told him he was my father and that I loved him with all my heart.

I still remember the day I told him that. When I looked up at him, he was staring at the small TV in the dining room with tears in his eyes. I didn't know what to do, so I ran under the kitchen table and hid. I lay there and ended up falling asleep.

I heard my mother when she walked into my grandparents' house. She joyfully screamed, *"Hello, what are you guys doing? Where's Natasha?"* As I started waking up, I heard my grandfather say, *"Shh, why do you have to be so loud? You're going to wake her up."* I thought to myself, *"Aww."* For people who knew my grandfather, he said very little but had a heavy presence. I lay there and smiled. Then I crawled out from under the table, rubbing my eyes as if I had just woken up. My grandfather said, *"See that, Carolvon, you woke her up."* My mother laughed, and I smiled.

I owe my grandfather a huge thank you for helping to shape me into who I am today. I have no regrets because I told him how I felt, and he showed me his love every day through the sacrifices he made. Toward the end of his days, I would give him a big kiss on the cheek, and he would close his eyes and sigh deeply. I would sometimes say, *"Let me give you a fat kiss,"* and he would lean his face over for one.

Writing this still brings tears to my eyes, and I've learned that if you love someone, you need to say it in the moment because we are not guaranteed tomorrow. Even showing appreciation by thanking someone for what they do matters. Telling someone now, while you have the chance, is important. Sometimes that other person needs to hear *"Thank you,"* *"I love you,"* or *"What you did meant a lot."* These words may help someone deal with the trials of life and limit regrets.

Two weeks before my grandfather passed away, my great-aunt, who had been staying next door with my grandmother's other sister for the past few months, passed away. She had become ill and came down to be with family who could care for her. Since I was home with my baby, my great-aunt would come over and spend time with us. I would drive her and my other great-aunt to stores and wherever they needed to go. My great-aunt V was something else. She always made me laugh, so driving around with them felt like hanging out with friends.

I remember one day, my sister and I snuck up on great-aunt V in the store and said, *"Boo."* She jumped and grabbed her bag. She said, *"Oh, you're lucky. I was about to go in my bag, grab my little tutu, and beat you over the head."* My sister almost fell on the floor laughing. She said, *"Tutu?"* Great-aunt V pulled out a miniature-sized hammer and said, *"Yeah, tutu,"* as she gestured as if hitting us in the head. I had tears in my eyes from laughing. She was such a sweet lady who didn't play when it came to defending herself. Aunt V said, *"I never go anywhere without my hammer."*

She loved sitting and holding my daughter as a baby. Soon, we learned that she had only a short time left with us. When she passed, it was on my birthday. I was glad we had shared time filled with love and laughter. That August was tough, especially for my grandmother. Losing her sister and then her husband two weeks later was heartbreaking.

The loss was hard for everyone in my family. It felt like each time I lost someone I loved, I emotionally withdrew from others. It was the start of my emotional unavailability, which grew with each passing loss in my family. Each loss was like a stone placed on my heart, slowly building a wall that made it difficult to reach out or be reached. I didn't realize that in trying to protect myself, I was isolating my heart from the love it needed. I still did not seek God, but I felt a strong urge to pray for and over my baby constantly. At the time, I didn't fully understand that the feeling was God providing guidance. It took some time for me to understand that the unshakable urge to pray was God's way of gently steering me back into His embrace, even when I was too hurt to see it.

Chapter 7: It Happened Again!

"Praise be to the God and Father of our Lord Jesus Christ, the Father of compassion and the God of all comfort, who comforts us in all our troubles, so that we can comfort those in any trouble with the comfort we ourselves receive from God."

— 2 Corinthians 1:3-4 (NIV)

* * *

As time passed, I started taking my daughter to church with me. She was around ten or eleven months old and would sit there quietly. Time flew by, and we settled into the same routine every Sunday for a few years. By now, she was around three years old. My daughter would sit next to me like a sweet, beautiful doll. At the end of the service, people would often ask if she had been there the entire time. I'd laugh and say, "Yes." The sweet sounds of gospel music would put her to sleep every time until the very end. In those moments, watching her rest peacefully in the sanctuary, I felt a glimmer of hope— a reminder that there was still a sense of calm amidst the storm of emotions I carried.

About three years after my great-aunt's passing, I continued taking my other great-aunt, who lived next door, grocery shopping. My daughter loved the ride, and my great-aunt thought my daughter was the cutest little girl. They enjoyed each other's company.

One day, my great-aunt said to me, "I need to have surgery done." I thought, Okay, you're over 70 years old. What surgery are you having? She explained that the doctor and his interns were concerned about her test results but assured her everything would be fine. He reassured her that it would be an in-and-out procedure, but something didn't feel right to me.

On the morning of my great-aunt's surgery, she rang the doorbell, and we all walked out to the hall. She said, "Alright, I'm off, and I'll be back soon." My mother told her to call when it was over and that we would stop by. I stood there, feeling weak and sick to my stomach. I had a strong feeling that this would be the last time we would see her. A nagging voice in my mind whispered that I should hug her, but I pushed it away, telling myself not to be dramatic. "It's just nerves," I thought. But deep down, I knew it was more. I didn't know why I felt that way, so I walked inside instead of giving her a hug.

We went back inside, and my mother continued preparing dinner for later. A few hours later, my daughter ran out of the living room into the kitchen and said, "She's dying, she's dying." I said, "Hey, don't say that." But my daughter insisted, "But Mommy, she is dying." It was unsettling to realize that my daughter, so young and innocent, had an intuition that echoed my own unspoken fears. It made me wonder if children, unburdened by the noise of doubt, could sense truths we adults tried to ignore. A wave of déjà vu hit me, reminding me of when I went to my other great-aunt's apartment as a child, and said the same thing to my mother about my great uncle.

I looked up, and my mother was staring at me. We didn't say a word. I picked my daughter up and said, "Everything will be alright." Shortly after, the phone rang, and my grandmother said someone needed to get to the hospital.

I quickly threw on my clothes and ran to the door. I saw my cousin, my great-aunt's grandson, getting into the car with his friend.

We raced to the hospital, where we were informed that there had been an accident during surgery. My great-aunt's blood pressure had dropped, and she passed away. I couldn't believe it. I didn't know what to say. I looked at my cousin and froze. His mother had been my cousin who passed away when he was young, and now he had lost both women in his life. I didn't want to say the typical "I'm so sorry." Instead, I just looked at him as tears streamed down my face.

I realized that I wasn't good at handling these situations. I would automatically shut down when someone died. I became numb and put on a "put-together" front. I didn't cry anymore; I just helped my mother gather the life insurance papers and make funeral arrangements—anything to avoid dealing with the reality. My relationships grew distant, as I feared allowing anyone too close might invite more pain. It was easier to stay numb, guarded by the walls I had carefully built. I bottled my feelings and pushed them away, becoming mechanical in my actions, while questions replayed in my mind every night.

There were so many questions. I started to feel angry, sad, guilty, and confused. Why did this keep happening? How did my daughter know? Where was God? What is going on? Who would be next? How would I handle it? These questions lingered in my mind, eroding my trust in God. I wanted answers, but feared what they might reveal. It was a time of spiritual limbo, where faith was both a lifeline and a source of confusion. I had to grieve quickly because time waited for no one.

Shortly after, I began searching for a home to purchase. It was time for me to move out. I found a co-op and was hesitant at first. Even though it was only ten blocks away—a five-minute drive—I didn't want to leave my mother. As I packed my things, the pain intensified. With each box sealed, I felt as though pieces of me were being ripped away from her. The series of events that had taken place filled me with fear, but I knew I had to keep moving forward.

At that time, I didn't know that moving was also a form of loss. Moving is considered emotionally traumatic at any stage of life. Research has shown that moving is among the top five most traumatic events, following behind the death of a loved one. This is because moving means leaving a place you have known as home for years. Change can be difficult for some, while it may be what others seek and need.

You are moving from somewhere familiar to an unknown place. Moving can be a happy event but may also bring fear and anxiety for some. It is crucial not to underestimate or ignore these feelings in both adults and children. Over the next decade or two, I would encounter several significant losses, including death and moving. I would later learn that these events shaped who I became and laid a new path for me to follow. Little did I know, these experiences were not just chapters of loss, but the foundation for a strength I would come to rely on. They were the seeds of a resilience I hadn't yet discovered.

Chapter 8: The Unthinkable

"As a mother comforts her child, so will I comfort you; and you will be comforted over Jerusalem."

— Isaiah 66:13 (NIV)

* * *

A few months after moving, unexplained medical issues started happening to my mother. She would occasionally complain of headaches. Years prior, she had received a machine for sleep apnea, and she had also hit her head in a car accident. The doctors couldn't determine what was causing the headaches. A few times, my mother mentioned that she didn't remember how she ended up in the basement or didn't realize she had to go to the bathroom. We insisted that she needed to see a doctor. Each day, the nagging worry in the pit of my stomach grew heavier– a silent alarm that kept going off in the background of my mind.

I'll never forget one particular day. My daughter was participating in a graduation ceremony for her preschool, which was just up the street from my mother's house. Although it wasn't her graduation year, she had a part in the ceremony and was all dressed up. Her little dress shimmered in the morning sunlight, and the excitement in her eyes sparkled like the glistening dew on the grass outside. She was filled to the brim with excitement to get to school and take part in her morning festivities. My mother, on the other hand, was moving rather slowly. Therefore, in an attempt to not delay the morning excitement, I told my mother I'd come back for her, after dropping my daughter off at school.

As promised, I returned back to the house to pick up my mother. However, she was nowhere to be found. I searched the basement, ran upstairs, and asked my grandmother and uncle if they had seen her. They said, "No, are you sure she's not downstairs?" I replied, "I'm sure." I got in my car and drove back up the street to see if she was walking. When I went inside the school, there she was, sitting and out of breath. Seeing her sitting there, I realized how fiercely determined she was to be present for every moment that mattered, even when her body resisted.

I couldn't believe it. I had told my mother I would come back to pick her up, but she thought I wouldn't because she was taking too long. At that moment, I had no idea what I would discover just a few months later. Innocently and naively, I thought it was no big deal since my daughter wasn't graduating that year. I assumed that my mother could wait until the following year. However, I didn't know that next year would never come for her to see her first grandchild graduate. It was a lesson that life, in all its uncertainty, offers moments we don't get to repeat, reminding me to cherish them while they're here. I'm so grateful she was there for that beautiful event.

Even though my mother passed away 12 years ago, telling this story makes it feel like it happened yesterday. My mother was a fair parent. The pain of her absence is still vivid, a reflection of the profound impact she had on my life and the countless memories that shaped who I am. Her influence was felt in the smallest moments, where fairness and love intertwined seamlessly. My mother was the kind of person who made sure that if she did for one, she did for all. She believed in equality not just as a principle, but as a way of nurturing and uplifting those around her. I had a close relationship with her. As a child, I never wanted to leave her side because I always felt like I was her protector. She was such a happy person, and I wanted to make sure she kept her smile. Despite her challenges, she wore her smile like armor. Little did I know, while I was trying to protect her, she was shielding us from the weight she carried so that we could feel safe and secure.

My mother would set up game nights on Fridays or Saturdays. She'd make pudding and homemade chocolate chip cookies, and even let us eat some raw cookie dough, every once in a while. If we ate too much, she'd yell, "You're going to end up with salmonella poisoning!" Of course, there were times when we got into trouble, and she would discipline us. But there was always a lesson to be learned, and we never repeated the same mistakes. To this day, the smell of warm cookies takes me back to those moments, filling me with a bittersweet ache for simpler times.

She was loving, patient, and kind-hearted. I remember her saying, "If you're going to do something for someone, make sure you do it without complaining. If you're going to complain while doing it, then don't do it at all." She always reminded us to have a praying heart, be good, never hate, and never be spiteful.

At bedtime, my mother would tuck us in and pray with us every night. She taught us how to pray and made sure we gave thanks to God. I also remember that, once in a while, late at night when she thought we were asleep, she'd go into the bathroom, shut the door, and cry. I could hear her. Each muffled sob felt like a weight pressing on my tiny chest, leaving me wide awake and helpless to ease her pain.

Raising three kids by herself was hard. Yes, we had our village of people in the house who loved us, but my mother felt like she had the weight of the world on her shoulders—and rightfully so. She wanted to give us everything she could and instill values and faith in God that we could carry throughout our lives. My mother wanted the best for us, and I wanted the best for her.

I know my mother never planned for her marriage to end in divorce. Sometimes, things happen, and that's her story to tell, not mine. Hearing her cry at night broke my heart. As a child, I felt that if I could just love her hard enough, it would take away her pain and struggles.

One night, I climbed down from my bunk bed and went to the bathroom door. I asked, "Why are you crying?" My mother replied, "Go to bed. I'm okay." I told her I wanted to hug and kiss her, and she said,

"Go to bed. I'll come to you when I'm finished." She composed herself, came to my bed, and I hugged and kissed her. "I love you so much," I said. "Thank you for being my mommy."

From that moment on, I decided I would be her protector. From that night forward, I would listen intently for any signs of distress, ready to jump into action even though I was just a child. My love was a shield I would wield fiercely, no matter how small I was. I thought, "If anyone ever tried to mess with her, that would be the last breath they'd take." I knew I was just a little girl, but I also knew that a little girl who loves her mother should never be underestimated.

Chapter 9: Saying Goodbye

"The Lord is close to the brokenhearted and saves those who are crushed in spirit."

— Psalm 34:18 (NIV)

* * *

After a series of unfortunate events, my mother ended up in the hospital. A sense of dread settled deep in my chest, the kind that whispers that life as you know it is about to change. The doctors finally discovered what was causing all the confusion she had been experiencing. I want to share this in case it can save a life: the doctors told us that my mother had an *absence seizure*. We were relieved because it could be treated with medication. I thought I finally had my mother back. For a brief moment, hope lit up our hearts, making us believe we could reclaim normalcy. However, that hope was interrupted. Just a day or two before she was supposed to come home, my mother complained to the doctor about her breathing.

The doctor recognized the problem immediately, prepared a crash cart and equipment, and rushed to take her to surgery. I had no idea what was happening. I had just finished work and was heading to the hospital when I bumped into my sister in the lobby. We were talking and laughing, completely unaware that this would be our last moment of happiness for another decade. It was as if God gave us one final gift before the storm.

When we stepped off the elevator, a nurse rushed up to us and said, "Pray, pray hard, and don't stop praying." I looked at her, confused. *What are you talking about?* I thought. Then I heard someone shout, "Code Blue, Code Blue." I looked down the hall and saw doctors racing with my mother's bed toward an elevator, my aunt running behind them, crying. The sound of hurried footsteps echoed down the corridor, mingling with the sterile scent of antiseptics and the frantic beeping of monitors.

We all ran into the elevator, and I was in shock. *What the hell is happening?* I thought. They rushed my mother into what I believe was the ICU and worked tirelessly to save her. My brother burst into the unit, shouting, "You have to fight, Ma." A sharp pain gripped my chest as I sank to the floor. One of my aunt's best friends grabbed me and urged me to be strong for my mother. I tried, but it felt like I was having a heart attack. I remember thinking, *Lord, please don't take me away from my daughter.*

The doctors managed to bring my mother back after two cardiac arrests. We were told that she had a blood clot, a pulmonary embolism, that had traveled to her heart. The doctors used a clot-busting medication to dissolve it, saving her life but causing her brain to bleed. The extent of the damage was unknown, and they didn't expect her to survive the night—or the weekend. My mother remained in the ICU for several weeks.

I prayed relentlessly for her every single day. The anticipatory grief was overwhelming, and for two weeks, I suffered from severe chest pain that I now know were anxiety attacks.

It became a constant battle with hospitals, doctors, and rehabilitation centers. I realized that compassion in healthcare was scarce. While there were some incredible nurses and a few dedicated doctors, they were rare. I understand that repeated exposure to death can lead to desensitization, but when you start to act like a robot and stop caring, it's time to step away. There were also doctors whose motives I questioned, but that's a story for another time.

Over time, my mother's health fluctuated. Each day was a cycle of hope, fear, and exhaustion– a relentless seesaw that wore down my heart. After a period of intensive outpatient therapy, she showed signs of improvement, even walking with assistance. But each time she made progress, she contracted another infection while in the hospital.

I also had a sense that something was wrong with the facility where she was staying. My mother couldn't speak or move on her own much due to the recurring infections. An employee confided in us that she didn't like how the staff treated my mother. We decided to bring her home, where she could be surrounded by love and protection.

Her condition continued to deteriorate. Watching her suffer was like being chained to the sidelines of a battle, unable to fight or flee– only endure. We watched her suffer slowly, trapped in her own body, sometimes able to open her eyes and speak or pray, but ultimately unable to do much. I felt helpless, watching my mother die a slow and painful death right before my eyes, unable to do anything but plead with God.

One evening, after caring for my mother, I returned home feeling defeated, angry, sad, and abandoned by God. My daughter and I went to bed after I said a prayer. Sometime during the night, I had a dream that my uncle visited me. I was shocked at first, then happy, and finally, sadness set in.

He said, "Don't worry anymore; your mother will be alright." His presence was almost celestial. *Was God answering my prayers?* I wondered. Only time will tell.

Time passed, and my mother's condition worsened. I started to question my dream. *What did it mean? Why did I have it?* It was as if the dream was a prelude to a farewell, a gentle reminder that God was preparing me, even if I refused to understand it. Four months later, the week of Mother's Day, my uncle appeared again in my dreams. This time, I wasn't afraid. I confronted him, asking, "What did you mean before when you said everything would be alright?" He tilted his head slightly and said, "It's time." My heart shattered.

I felt that same crushing pain in my chest as I did when my mother first went into cardiac arrest. I managed to choke out, "What do you mean?" He looked at me with sympathy and repeated, "It's time."

I woke up, crying uncontrollably. We went to the hospital to visit my mother, and all I could do was hold her. She was unconscious and had been for a few days. Her body was tired; she was transitioning. On Mother's Day, my mother passed away. The day meant to honor mothers became the day I lost mine, forever changing the meaning of Mother's Day.

We went through the motions of the funeral and tried to carry on with life. I felt empty and angry at God for not saving her. I was bitter because she had been so caring and deserved better than the painful death she endured. I walked away from God. Whatever He wanted, I did the opposite. I didn't care who I hurt in my relationships. *Hurt people hurt people*—and I was no exception.

I resented my father, too. Why did she sacrifice so much and suffer while he, who hadn't been around, could now reap the benefits of what she had instilled in us? My mother always wanted us to have a relationship with him, but I didn't care anymore. I stopped going to church and cried myself to sleep every night for a year. If God was love, why did He let my heart break so completely? The question echoed in my soul, unanswered and heavy.

One snowy day, about nine months after my mother's passing, I picked up my daughter and headed home. The snow suddenly turned into a blizzard. I stopped at a red light and had a flashback of my uncle teaching me to watch the walk signal to know when the light would change.

As I glanced at the walk signal, a car slammed into the back of my Jeep. The impact was so strong that the vehicle lifted. I reached back instinctively to protect my daughter. We always wore seatbelts, but you can never be too sure.

The accident led to surgery and months of rehab. I could barely walk, and the doctors refused to give me a walker, fearing my legs would weaken more. The pain was unbearable, and I used the time to grieve even more for my mother.

I realized later that my daughter grieved with me. She would wake up in the middle of the night to check on me. Looking back, I see how my grief affected her, amplifying her own grief. Untreated grief opened doors to anger, isolation, sickness, and a life without faith. I became emotionally unavailable and tired of loving only to lose. For a decade, I was so blinded by pain that I didn't realize God had been with me all along, even in my dreams. It took years for me to realize that the same grief that isolated me was also the key to understanding the depth of God's quiet presence.

Chapter 10: You Saved My Life

"And we know that in all things God works for the good of those who love him, who have been called according to his purpose."

— Romans 8:28 (NIV)

* * *

D ays and months passed, and I remained unchanged. I remember watching a commercial about someone who appeared to be functioning well despite being deeply depressed. To the world, everything seemed perfectly normal for this person—they got up, went to work, smiled, and laughed, making others believe they were alright.

Internally, my soul told a different story. My soul was like a weary traveler, navigating through a maze with no clear exit. Each day felt like walking on shattered glass, trying not to fall apart. It was as if my inner being stood on a faulty foundation—a place riddled with cracks, missing pieces, and gaping holes. There was darkness, but small glimpses of light shone through. That light was my daughter. In the darkest corners of my grief, her laughter was like a lifeline, tethering me to a reality that still held glimpses of hope. Sometimes, my soul would reach for that light to gain energy, allowing joy to seep in and making me appear fully present.

With that grief came an urge for control. Since I couldn't control what had happened to the loved ones I lost, I decided to control as much of my life as I could. I revisited the plans I had made years ago and reviewed the list of goals I wanted to achieve by certain ages and dates. Each unchecked box on that list was a reminder of time lost and dreams deferred. It gnawed at me, fueling a cycle of frustration and self-doubt, as I felt I had missed my deadlines.

I enrolled in graduate school, passed my exams, and completed my second master's degree, but I still wasn't happy. I was upset that I didn't own a house and only had a co-op. Despite having so much, I felt empty and unfulfilled. Something important was missing, but I couldn't figure out what. I wanted to give my daughter the fairy tale life I had read about and seen in movies. Nothing I did made me happy, and I definitely wasn't grateful—I was still angry at God.

I was weighed down by unanswered questions and deep sadness, but through it all, God pulled me through. One night, I had a dream that I will never forget for as long as I live. I was in a place that resembled a hospital. The waiting area was bright, almost as if light was bouncing off mirrored walls.

I saw flashes of a dress as white as snow, with beautiful brown arms and legs moving gracefully. When my eyes adjusted, I saw it was my mother. A wave of happiness washed over me, and tears filled my eyes. I ran to hug her. Her embrace was warm, like stepping into a sunbeam on a chilly day. The familiar scent of her favorite perfume wrapped around me, evoking a flood of childhood memories.

She twirled around, holding the bottom of her dress and moving joyfully. "Look at my feet! I can walk again. Look, I'm dancing," she said, laughing. It had been so long since I'd heard her laugh—her illness had taken that from her. My mother was full of joy! For a moment, I forgot all about the pain and heartache. Seeing her so alive made everything else fall away, if only for a few fleeting seconds.

"I miss you, Mom," I said through my tears. She smiled and told me she knew I missed her, but that I shouldn't worry anymore. After a brief conversation, she said she had to go. I asked where she was going, thinking she had another doctor's appointment, still unable to understand why I was in a hospital. She laughed and said, "No, I don't need any more doctor appointments, but you do." Confused, I asked, "What do you mean?" She just smiled and said, "Make sure you go to the doctor," and told me she loved me.

I woke up the next morning and immediately scheduled doctor appointments. Most things checked out fine, but the doctor noted some issues with my stomach caused by stress. It was just beginning, and I knew I needed to address it. Seeing my mother in that dream and knowing she was alright began to soften my heart. The healing process started slowly, but I felt peace knowing she was at rest. It was as if a small, long-locked door inside me had cracked open, allowing slivers of acceptance and hope to seep through.

After that dream, I started going back to church for my daughter's sake. I knew that my feelings toward God should not impact her, and I wanted her to have the chance to form her own relationship with Him. I promised myself that my pain would not be her inheritance; she deserved a foundation rooted in love and faith, not bitterness. I wanted to build a new spiritual foundation for her, so I began looking for a church to join. The groundwork was always there—she had been in religious schools since she was two and a half years old until she graduated from high school.

One evening at a Girl Scout meeting, while the mothers waited in the hallway, a conversation about church came up. One mother suggested I visit her church in New Jersey. Since we lived close to the state line, it wasn't a big deal. She had invited me before, but at the time, my mother was still alive, and my sister and I were her caretakers. This time, after my mother's passing, I agreed that we might visit over the summer.

A few weeks later, a former coworker stopped by my job to say hello. She offered her condolences and asked how I was doing. She told me about a new church she had joined in New Jersey and encouraged me to visit. I shared this with a friend, who said, "Wait, my coworker mentioned a church in Jersey too, and suggested we visit." It seemed like more than coincidence. Could it be the same church?

Finally, summer came, and we decided to attend the church. The service was incredible, and I cried my eyes out. It felt as if the sermon was written just for me. Afterward, we lingered in the grand lobby, catching up with familiar faces. Suddenly, I bumped into the Girl Scout mother who had originally invited me. We laughed and marveled at the small world moment. I told everyone the story, and someone said, "This is nothing but God!"

It was in that moment I knew it was time to take my life back. We continued attending services at the Community Baptist Church of Englewood for a few years. My daughter joined Sunday school, and we participated in church activities. One sermon spoke directly to me: "If you are carrying the weight of worries, sadness, stress, or burdens, it's time to lay that cross at the altar and give it to God."

I walked to the altar more than once, each time thinking it would be my last. I prayed for God to help me find my way, but I struggled to stay consistent. I still had so many questions and lingering pain. I was trying my best to heal, but it wasn't until one Sunday that everything changed.

For weeks, my daughter had been telling me how much she enjoyed sitting in the sanctuary and listening to the sermons. One Sunday, instead of attending Sunday school, she sat with us. At the end of the service, the pastor asked if anyone wanted to give their life to God. My daughter, about 11 or 12 at the time, leaned over and said, "Mom, I want to walk down to the altar."

Then, she stood up and said, "Mom, I'm walking down to the altar." I jumped up and followed her. There was no way I would let her walk alone. That moment of supporting her turned into me recommitting my life to God. It felt like the first step on a long bridge I hadn't realized I was building— a bridge that spanned the chasm between loss and hope.

God truly works through children to reach adults. I realized that sometimes, God's voice isn't heard in grand gestures or miracles but in the simple, unguarded moments shared with those we love. That day, my daughter saved my life. The dedication of this book says, "You saved my life," and now you know why. Her decision to give her life to God led me to say, "Yes, I want to believe again. I want to live again." From that day on, my life changed. The road to healing was still long and winding, but now I had my daughter's hand in mine and faith in God to guide me forward.

Chapter 11: New Season

"Call to me and I will answer you and tell you great and unsearchable things you do not know."

— Jeremiah 33:3 (NIV)

* * *

In this new season of my life, I embarked on an incredible journey toward peace. I intentionally sought different avenues to build a closer relationship with God. In my private moments, I would ask God to help me understand Him better. I would sit quietly in my room, the hum of the world fading into the background, yearning for a connection that felt just out of reach. I wanted to hear His voice. I even promised God I wouldn't pass out if He spoke to me. Deep down, I knew my heart would race with the kind of awe that only God can evoke, but I was ready—or so I told myself. But could you imagine hearing a deep, rumbling voice? My knees would probably buckle, and I'd collapse. All I asked was to be either sitting or lying down before He started talking.

I prayed, prayed, and prayed some more for a breakthrough. It wasn't until COVID-19 hit that a friend introduced me to two women who were prophets. They hosted various online events and occasionally shared prophetic words. Between church and these events, things started to fall into place for a while. There were days when it felt like I was on the edge of a breakthrough, but just as quickly, that feeling would dissolve. Instead, that nagging feeling of something missing crept back in. I felt like I needed more. Once again, I spoke to God, saying, "Father, you know me, and you know I don't want to wait for a prophetic word to hear from you. Why won't you speak to me?"

At that point, I committed to spending more time in the Word. I prayed and asked God to guide me to a version of the Bible I could understand—one that wouldn't put me to sleep. "Father," I said, "I want to learn your Word, but every time I open the Bible, I fall asleep."

I attended a spiritual conference with an amazing group of women I had followed online. I trusted these women were of God because one of my friends attended church with one of them and had known her for years. The atmosphere was filled with anticipation, as worship music played softly in the background. The women's voices carried a mixture of excitement and reverence, creating an atmosphere that felt both holy and energizing.

After we arrived and settled in, the prophetess approached me and said, "God wants me to let you know He is going to send you a Bible you can understand." My heart thudded in my chest, with a mixture of disbelief and exhilaration surging through me. It felt as though God had read my private journal and was answering my hidden prayers. I was instantly shocked, feeling like a child caught in a fib. My immediate thought was, "Uh-oh, you did it now." It hit me then that God knew I was bluffing when I said I wouldn't faint if He spoke to me. At that moment, I wanted to pass out. It was a mixture of awe and humility— knowing that God had not only heard my words, but had chosen to respond directly through someone else. All I could manage to say was, "Alright," with eyes wide in astonishment.

The prophetess continued, "God wants you to know that you hear Him, but you're so distracted by everything around you that you don't realize it." At that moment, it hit me—God had seen me open my Bible at night and fall asleep on it. Oh, Lord!

Sure enough, I searched online and found the Bible she mentioned. A wave of warmth washed over me, as I clicked through the pages online. It came in a pink floral cover—my favorite color. The floral cover seemed to smile back at me like an answered prayer. As soon as I previewed it, I knew it was from God. I ordered it, and from the day it arrived, I couldn't put it down. I turned its pages as though I were reading an enthralling novel. The stories were filled with more drama than any TV show and resonated deeply with me.

I became intentional with my time. Each moment spent in quiet reflection felt like laying a stone on the path back to myself—solid, steady, and blessed. I stopped spending hours on the phone discussing trivial matters and instead focused on reading the Bible or lying quietly, imagining I was resting in my Heavenly Father's arms. I would fall asleep listening to praise and worship music. Sure enough, I began to hear God's voice. He came to me in dreams, often appearing as my uncle. I think He knew I felt safe with Him.

I used to walk around believing that whatever could go wrong, would go wrong. God told me to stop that negative thinking and to speak positively about myself. It was as if I had been carrying an umbrella, always expecting rain, but God showed me the beauty of stepping into the sun. From that point forward, I reclaimed my confidence and faith—the very qualities the enemy had tried to steal from me. I began walking in unwavering, supernatural faith.

One important lesson I learned from sermons and conferences was that limiting distractions and setting aside time with God allows you to hear Him. I have countless testimonies. For instance, when I felt a heaviness in my stomach and a strong prompting to see my doctor, I listened. I had already seen most of my doctors but remembered there was one left. Following the Holy Spirit's nudge, I went to see him, and thank God I did! My doctor discovered cells that were on the verge of becoming cancerous, and I had surgery just in time. It was a strong reminder that God's divine guidance is more than whispers of comfort —it is a call to act and safeguard the life He gifted. Truly, learning to listen to God can be the difference between life and death.

Chapter 12: Parenting Children Dealing with Grief

"Train up a child in the way he should go, and when he is old, he will not depart from it."

— Proverbs 22:6 (NKJV)

* * *

S upporting children through grief is deeply meaningful to me because I have seen firsthand how, if left unaddressed, grief can profoundly shape a child's entire life.. If you have a child, teaching them where to turn in times of need is critical for their well-being. Teaching your children how to seek God and access professional counseling is essential.

When my family experienced multiple losses, my daughter shared that pain. Between the ages of four and eighteen, she faced the loss of my mother, her great-uncle, her great-grandmother on her father's side, her great-grandmother on my mother's side, and another great-uncle. One loss, in particular, struck especially hard.

My Uncle David was a very special man. During the time my mother was sick, my uncle, who was my daughter's great-uncle, lived upstairs with my grandmother and took care of her. He saw how difficult it was for my sister and me to care for my mother, so he offered to pick my daughter up from school every day. This allowed me to work a few hours of overtime without having to rush to get her and then return to work before caring for my mother. My uncle and my daughter had such a blessed relationship. She was about six years old and had him wrapped around her little finger. They would often playfully argue over who was going to pay for lunch or a treat.

One year before my mother passed away, my uncle passed away. It hit us hard! My daughter didn't have her great-uncle anymore; her best friend was gone. When I spoke of my uncle coming to me in my dreams, this was the uncle I refer to. His passing left a void that resonated throughout our family, especially for my daughter. The impact of losing him was compounded by the memories she had with other cherished family members who had also passed.

My daughter spent time with each of her beloved relatives at different stages of her life, forming close bonds with them. They shared moments filled with laughter, stories, and love—memories that became both her comfort and her source of pain when they were gone. When they passed away, I would ask her if she was alright. Of course, as a child, she would say, "Yes," but I knew it was challenging for her.

I told myself I would be mindful of her actions to see if grief started to set in. But life happened, and one event after another kept me from watching for the signs. Over time, I began to see anxiety building up and a sense of overwhelm creeping in. It was then that I realized that grief had woven itself into her daily life, manifesting in small, almost imperceptible ways until it couldn't be ignored. It hit me that I needed to let my daughter speak with a grief counselor. Each session uncovered emotions that had been tucked away, revealing just how deeply grief had embedded itself in her young heart. I knew this wouldn't be a quick process— it took time, much like peeling the layers of an onion. However, the journey was essential, each step bringing her closer to healing and understanding.

For privacy reasons, I won't share any of her personal experiences, as it's not my story to tell. What I will share are practical steps for seeking help. If you have insurance, it is best to use it rather than paying out of pocket. The process can be tedious because many counselors operate on an out-of-pocket basis and don't accept insurance. During that time, it was especially important for me to find a provider of the same ethnicity and a female, so my daughter would feel comfortable sharing.

Reviewing their specialties, expertise, and treatment approach is essential. This ensures that your child receives the specific support they need to navigate their unique grief journey. You also want to ensure that the provider has the appropriate experience, much like choosing a cardiologist for heart issues rather than visiting a podiatrist or dermatologist. Finding support tailored to your specific needs is crucial.

Grief is intense and affects many aspects of life. A person may experience sadness, anger, guilt, and other emotions. They may also experience anticipatory grief, mourning someone who is still alive. This is why finding a specialist who understands the stages of grief is so important. The process is ongoing, which is why it's beneficial to find someone who accepts your medical plan.

You don't want to start paying out of pocket only to realize later that you can no longer afford it. Interruptions in service or changing providers midway through the process are not ideal because they often require starting over. If a change is necessary, it's better to address it early and be proactive.

A skilled counselor or therapist will not only let you express your feelings, but will also discuss strategies to manage them daily when grief becomes overwhelming. This might include journaling, creating a grief calendar, or engaging in therapeutic activities to process emotions. This skilled individual will also help you explore how grief impacts different areas of your life: moving, changing schools, jobs, friendships, death, relationships, and more. Over time, unresolved feelings can accumulate and cause further issues.

Introducing your children to God is also vital. While attending church and participating in ministry are beneficial, building a personal relationship with God is transformative. A relationship with God can become their source of comfort when life feels overwhelming, teaching them to seek solace in His unwavering presence. Teaching your children to read and understand the Word of God can change the trajectory of their lives. I am careful about endorsements because we are all human and flawed. Yet, I grew spiritually with the help of what I call "destiny helpers"—people who followed and obeyed God's Word.

I once learned about breaking generational curses through a 25-day fast led by a well-known prophetess. I asked God for help, and He answered, as He always does. With teachings from this prophetess and a pastor, I developed a stronger relationship with God. My daughter and I did everything together, whether it was fasting, praying, or reading Scripture. These moments strengthened not only our relationship with God, but also our bond as mother and daughter, creating a foundation of mutual trust and spiritual resilience. This process was important for us to do as a team. We learned to read and apply God's Word. We are our children's first role models, and they learn by watching us.

Through this journey, I learned to exercise authority over my emotions and reactions. The scales fell from my eyes, granting me deeper discernment. My daughter learned to pray using Scripture and intentionally speak to God about everything. Over time, God answered her questions—sometimes immediately, sometimes later.

She learned to be patient and developed spiritual discernment. It was as if she was reborn. During grief counseling, we discovered how grief affects every facet of life and the importance of addressing it to prevent long-term negative effects.

Some people are entirely against counseling, therapy, and even God. Yet continuing to navigate life alone, without seeking guidance, is, in my view, true insanity. Seeking help doesn't mean you're weak; it means you're strong enough to take steps toward healing. As Believers, we know that not all battles are ours to fight. During my time of restoration, I learned that many battles occur in the spiritual realm. While we can handle some, others require God's intervention. This, however, is a subject for another day.

Sometimes we expect God to do everything for us and question why things go wrong. But God often sends help; we just don't recognize it. Recognizing the ways in which He answers prayers—whether through people, experiences, or gentle nudges—is part of growing spiritually. There is a parable about a man stranded at sea after a shipwreck. He prayed for God to save him, but when a boat, a helicopter, and the coast guard came, he declined their help, saying he was waiting for God.

When he died and went to heaven, he asked God why He didn't save him. God responded, "I sent you a boat, a helicopter, and the coast guard, but you refused them."

God often sends help in forms we don't expect. It's up to us to accept it. Teaching children to have a relationship with God shows them that He may send help through dreams, Bible verses, counseling, or other means.

Carefully selecting a therapist who can help your children process their emotions—and sometimes yours—is invaluable. Talking to your children without judgment, listening to their feelings, and asking how they feel without inserting your own perspective are key. Consider creating a safe space at home where they feel encouraged to share their thoughts, perhaps through designated "heart-to-heart" conversations.

As a teenager, I was fortunate to have a mother who never judged me. She taught me to pray and assured me that she would never judge my thoughts or feelings. She didn't just say it—she lived it.

Chapter 13: Walking in a Fog

"Trust in the Lord with all your heart and lean not on your own understanding; in all your ways submit to him, and he will make your paths straight."

— Proverbs 3:5-6 (NIV)

* * *

I have to admit that part of my struggles stemmed from my inability to let go and let God. I wanted to control every aspect of my life. This need for control was rooted in the many losses I had endured. My desire to control everything led me to make decisions I wouldn't normally make. This need for control created a constant tension in my life, leaving me feeling exhausted and disconnected from true peace. When I decided to give God my complete *yes*, I knew what that commitment would require.

It would mean trusting God's word without question. While I believed in God, my control issues were still there. Ultimately, they came down to my level of faith not being where it needed to be. I often ignored the signs God sent me, whether they came through the actions of others or a feeling of discomfort within myself. I *chose* to overlook those signs because I was afraid— afraid of what it would mean to let go of control and fully trust in God.

Every morning, I would wake up with stomach pains and a feeling of sickness once I reached my job. I worked there for over 19 years, and deep down, I understood what the pains were about. The sickness I felt was a spiritual battle. It was like a weight, making every breath feel labored and heavy. Each morning, I would pray and listen to praise and worship music on my drive to work to help ease the anxiety. The closer I grew to God, the more intense the pain became. My inner spirit and the spirit of one particular colleague seemed to clash. I began to see the darkness some people carried, and it was toxic.

At that moment, my dreams of holding a leadership position to support the children in that place faded. I realized it was time to leave a job I had invested in for nearly two decades. Doubt crept in as I thought about leaving the only professional environment I had known. Was I making a mistake, or was this God's way of nudging me toward a better path? It was time to trust God fully and follow His guidance. God had shown me signs long before that it was time to move on. So, I applied for another job and resigned from the place that had been a significant part of my life for so long.

I knew leaving would mean walking in a fog. This uncertainty was both terrifying and liberating, a strange paradox that I had to embrace. By "fog," I mean stepping into an unknown path, where visibility was limited and I had to rely solely on God, not on my own understanding. I didn't know what life would hold for me after resigning and moving out of state, but I was okay with that because I had given God my YES. I said, "Father, I will trust You completely. I will go wherever You lead me because I know You will protect and provide for me." I had no idea what the future held.

During this period, I began letting go of things that were not of God. I used to be known as the "Queen of the Curse Out." Although I was friendly, crossing me had consequences. I learned not to let other people's actions control my emotions. Now, instead of reacting with anger, I found myself pausing, breathing, and choosing grace. The grace God extended to me became the same grace I extended to others. I could see people clearly for who they were. Previously, I could sense certain things and discern some struggles people faced, but now, my vision was clear and my heart was softened. There were moments when someone tried to provoke me, but instead of responding with sharp words, I smiled and walked away. Although they were small victories, they were significant signs of growth.

When I gave God my YES and fully surrendered to Him, I didn't flinch, worry, or second-guess myself. I trusted that my Father would catch me. Walking in a fog means intentionally listening, observing, feeling, and trusting the process. It means embracing the discomfort of stepping into something new, while knowing that trust in the Lord is essential. It taught me that obedience isn't passive—it's an active choice to lean into faith, even when doubt whispers louder than hope.

God's timing is so different from ours. I often felt like I went to sleep, woke up, and discovered an entire decade of my life had passed. Part of that was due to caring for my mother, something I would do over and over if needed. Time also slipped away during my years of grieving. This caused me to feel anxious because so many of my plans had not materialized. But saying *yes* to God and walking in the fog allowed Him to restore everything. If you are facing a season of uncertainty, know that trusting in God's plan may feel like stepping into the unknown, but it is in that space where true miracles happen.

"And I will restore to you the years that the locust hath eaten, the cankerworm, and the caterpillar, and the palmerworm, my great army which I sent among you. You will have plenty to eat, until you are full, and you will praise the name of the Lord your God, Who has worked wonders for you; never again will my people be shamed. Then you will know that I am in Israel, that I am the Lord your God, and that there is no other; never again will my people be shamed."

— Joel 2:25-27 (KJV)

"Restoration! In Jesus' name, Amen!" I began to shout this with joy because I knew God would restore everything. I will continue to follow His voice and walk in the fog, for that trust and faith are far better than any anxious, controlling feeling I have ever experienced. Take a moment to look back on your own life and recognize how far you've come, even when the road seemed unclear.

Chapter 14: Healing

"He heals the brokenhearted and binds up their wounds."

— Psalm 147:3 (NIV)

* * *

B efore I gave God my complete *yes*, I spoke to Him, asking for healing and guidance toward a better, renewed life. I had that conversation with Him and slowly started to feel and see changes within me. What initially seemed like a gradual process soon accelerated to warp speed.

God began sending me destiny helpers—people who would guide me to a higher level in areas such as my prayer life and understanding His Word. As one person came into my life, another would follow, continuing the process. It wasn't a coincidence; it was God.

The joy and gratitude I feel as I write this are almost overwhelming. Reflecting on the journey of being filled and restored brings such an incredible sense of thankfulness. Praise be to God for His grace and mercy! I am so thankful for His unending grace and unconditional love, and I hope you feel encouraged to experience that same connection and gratitude in your own life.

As I wrote this book, I went back and forth, wondering if I should share deeply or hold back and keep most of my life lessons private. However, the deeper I immersed myself in gratitude, the more I realized that healing required honesty—not just with God, but with myself and others. So, I decided that if I was going to testify to how God brought me through, I needed to open up more. The healing process was challenging, as it required me to look not only at the wrongs others had done to me but also at the wrongs I had done to others and myself. It was time to release those feelings and let God handle them.

In the chapter "Seeds," I spoke about my first love. This relationship was part of my healing process. For too long, I held myself accountable for the pain I caused both of us. We both moved on, but deep down, I had not forgiven myself. While it wasn't intentional, some of my decisions were selfish, and I tried to play both sides at times. He was the first man, outside of my grandfather and uncle, whom I could say, without a doubt, loved me.

To my first love—if you happen to read this book—I am truly sorry for the pain I caused. Even though it was two decades ago, it mattered to me because the love was real. We are now different people living separate lives, but it was time for me to let go of this guilt. Letting go of this guilt is a release that makes space for peace. I hurt you publicly, so I am apologizing publicly.

I also want to apologize to those I didn't have direct contact with but who were affected by my actions. To friends who never received an explanation for why I stopped speaking to you—there were reasons. Sometimes silence was my only refuge, a way to shield myself from frustration I couldn't yet articulate. At the time, I didn't know how to express my feelings or how to say, "I don't like your behavior."

To know me is to know that any relationship I had was genuine. God places people in our lives for different reasons and seasons. Sometimes, we outgrow each other, and that's okay.

To those who wronged me—I forgive you. Every experience and every hurt has shaped who I am today. The heat and pressure were necessary for my transformation. This spiritual journey has taught me that. Forgiveness turned my pain into a lesson, shifting my mindset from victimhood to victory.

As a child, I heard bits and pieces about the spiritual realm. Sometimes, we visited different churches, and I witnessed people being delivered. Spiritual deliverance is the act of casting out evil spirits or demons. Once delivered, people replace those negative spirits with God's Word and the Holy Spirit. I didn't fully understand this as a child.

As an adult, I would sometimes wonder, "How can people be so cruel?" My grandmother would always say, "Oh, he ain't got nothing but the devil in him." Back then, I didn't realize she meant that

Anger is one of the most destructive spirits. During my healing process, I had to let go of the anger I held—from people abusing my trust, from relationships that failed, and from not walking away from certain jobs and situations when I should have. I allowed anger to take up residence within me for too long.

Despite my challenges, I had an amazing life filled with lessons and preparation. I had friends and family I loved fiercely. But that fierce love sometimes fueled my anger when things went wrong. I poured everything into what I did, and when it fell apart, I felt betrayed. If you find yourself in a similar battle, remember that recognizing these patterns is the first step toward healing.

As I revisited past relationships, I realized that each one was for a season and had its purpose. Although I only dated a few people, each relationship felt like it could have worked if timing or circumstances were different.

One relationship, in particular, should have ended much sooner. I continued it because we had fun, but deep down, I knew it wasn't going anywhere. When it finally ended, I gained clarity. Shortly after, I met someone new, but the timing wasn't right, and that relationship also ended.

After healing, I learned not to hold on to anything that doesn't produce forward movement. Before, I would replay events and think, "You knew better than to do that." God had warned me in subtle ways, but I ignored the signs because I was tired of always doing the right thing.

Now, I look back and see that my actions came from a place of hurt.

If you're revisiting your own story, be kind to yourself. Healing doesn't happen overnight, but every small step matters. Healing meant taking accountability for that hurt, not just the pain others caused me, but the pain I inflicted on myself and others. I sincerely apologize to those I hurt. If I told you I loved you, it was genuine.

I turned to work and shopping to bury my pain. Success made me feel accomplished, and shopping brought temporary joy. But nothing truly quenched my thirst until I returned to God. The Bible teaches that only the Holy Spirit can cleanse our souls and quench our spiritual thirst.

It took time, but I learned to appreciate every relationship and thank God for the lessons. Each experience, good or bad, built my character and strength. When I reflected on my journey, Genesis 50:20 came to mind: *"You intended to harm me, but God intended it for good to accomplish what is now being done, the saving of many lives."* What the enemy meant for evil, God used for my good.

Healing allowed me to address wounds I didn't realize I had. I had to let go of blaming my father and even my mother. My grief was real, and it was time to choose life—for myself and my daughter.

I encourage you to take time for yourself. Reflect on past events and how they've shaped you. Write down what emotions they evoke and how they impact your outlook. Be gentle with yourself and remember: it's okay to make mistakes. Take time to pamper and love yourself. Create affirmations, vision boards, and set achievable goals. Pray, read the Bible, and seek counseling, if needed. Above all, choose to love yourself.

Chapter 15: Giving Thanks

"Give thanks to the Lord, for he is good; his love endures forever."

— Psalm 107:1 (NIV)

* * *

"Walking in the fog" was an analogy that resonated deeply with me, as Tasha Cobbs so powerfully expressed on her live album. Throughout my healing journey, worship music became my daily companion, and walking in the fog perfectly described how I navigated life. In the early stages of this new chapter, I learned to walk without clear sight, relying solely on His voice to guide me. I have witnessed countless miracles in my life—moments where I should have died, but God's grace spared me. Although I always thanked God when I was younger, living through trauma has taught me to give thanks in a profoundly different way. What once felt like a simple gesture became a lifeline, a way to remind myself of God's steadfast presence even in the darkest hours.

Father, thank You for waking me up and giving me the strength to wash my own body. Thank You, Lord Jesus, for blessing me with a sound mind, knowing so many others will wake up today without one. Father, thank You for allowing me to walk freely, unassisted and independent. Thank You for never leaving me, even when I felt utterly alone after my mother passed away. You were there, even when I was too angry and broken to feel Your presence.

Thank You for Your grace and mercy. Thank You for loving me unconditionally. Father, I give You all the praise and all the glory. None of this would have been possible without You. Because of Your grace, I was able to achieve five degrees while being a single mom, caring for my mother physically, emotionally, and mentally, and maintaining a demanding career as an educator. Thank You, Lord, for giving me the strength to work after-school programs, weekends, and summers. Thank You for making a way for my daughter to be with me during those times when I worked—something not every employer would allow. And Father, I thank You for sending destiny helpers.

Thank You for allowing my mother to care for my daughter as an infant while I pursued my first master's degree. Thank You for my grandmother, who stepped in to care for my daughter so I could return to work. My daughter, with her strong-willed personality, made it clear that only her "fab four" could watch her, even if only for a short time.

Thank You, Father, for my uncle, who stepped in to help pick up my daughter so I could continue caring for my mother alongside my sister. Thank You for my daughter's preschool teacher, who was also her great-grandmother. Father, thank You for allowing all these incredible people to be part of my daughter's life before they passed away.

I see pieces of loved ones in her every day, and I am grateful for that. I magnify Your name, Lord. I am at a point in my life where I am intentional about my worship time, my boundaries, my feelings, and my overall life. Thank You, Heavenly Father, for allowing me to come into Your presence and for welcoming me.

Right now, take a moment to think about everything you're thankful for. Think of the moments that seemed insignificant but, in hindsight, were pivotal. What small blessings do you often overlook?

If you find yourself weary—tired of repeating the same behaviors and facing the same outcomes—try God. I'm not necessarily saying start by going to church (though finding a good church is a blessing), but understand that what God desires most is a personal relationship with you. Don't let your soul remain spiritually thirsty. Spiritual thirst is real. I didn't fully understand how parched my soul was until I felt the refreshing peace that only God's presence can bring. Talk to Him—humbly and with respect. Remember, He is not just a Father, but Almighty God.

Too often, people justify their choices by saying, "He knows my heart," and use that as an excuse to live a life that is not aligned with God's will. But think about it: would you want your own children to live in confusion, disregarding your guidance? No. So why would God, your Father, be alright with His child living that way?

God wants you to come as you are, but with the intent to be cleansed and renewed. Approach Him with love and humility. Seek Him earnestly and speak to Him from your heart.

Chapter 16: Forgiveness

"Be kind and compassionate to one another, forgiving each other, just as in Christ God forgave you."

— Ephesians 4:32 (NIV)

* * *

Forgiveness is the process of releasing feelings of anger and resentment toward someone who has harmed or wronged you. It is not about accepting their behavior or pretending that everything is fine. Forgiveness means letting go of the pain, hurt, and sadness and allowing God to handle the rest. In *Matthew 6:14-15* (NIV), the Bible states, "For if you forgive other people when they sin against you, your heavenly Father will also forgive you. But if you do not forgive others their sins, your Father will not forgive your sins."

Forgiveness is about walking in God's word. It might be a family member or even an employer that you need to forgive. Forgiveness is God's grace, a pathway for healing and breaking the cycle of anger and hatred. So, who do you need to forgive today? What did they do, and how did it affect your view of life? More importantly, how can you grow and rise above it?

I have forgiven many people and pray that those I may have hurt also forgive me. Forgiveness does not require face-to-face interaction. You can be in your room and say, "Father, I forgive [name] for blocking my growth at work" or "I forgive [name] for betraying me." Then, take the time to acknowledge your own mistakes by saying, "Father, please forgive me for my sins," and state them.

I found it helpful to speak out loud what I was forgiving people for: "I forgive you for trying to stand in my way." As I spoke those words, I realized something powerful—no person can prevent what God has planned for me. What is meant for me will always be mine. I forgive you for your attempts to block me, and I forgive myself for the anger I allowed to take root. You played into the enemy's plans, but I ultimately did what God called me to do.

I thank God for the closed doors that kept me from harm. As the saying goes, "What you meant for harm, God turned for my good." In *Genesis 50:20* (NIV), Joseph tells his brothers, "You intended to harm me, but God intended it for good to accomplish what is now being done, the saving of many lives."

It is true that we are human and live in the flesh, making it difficult to forgive certain events or people. There were times when the hurt was so deep that forgiving felt impossible. However, it is vital for our well-being. Forgiveness is not for the other person—it is a gift to ourselves, a path to healing and peace of mind. Holding onto that anger felt like carrying a heavy burden. I didn't realize how much it was affecting my daily interactions until I decided to let go and allow God to work through me.

Forgiveness is a journey that doesn't happen overnight. It takes time, and that's okay. Acknowledge the process and commit to it. I want to emphasize that I love my father, and sharing my story is not meant to cause harm, but to bring understanding and peace.

Some relationships require rebuilding, and I am willing to work on them as needed. However, know that just because I may not reach out frequently, it doesn't mean I am not thinking of you. It means I am learning to "walk again"—taking small steps at times, and big leaps at others. One day, a prophet gave me a message from God: "Forgive him. Your father was the vessel used to bring you into this world, but I am your Father, and I am here to protect and provide for you." That word was powerful. It reminded me that God has always been my ultimate protector and provider, and for that, I am grateful.

In my journey, forgiveness reached down into my deepest, most personal grief. When my mother passed, I felt a whirlwind of emotions. I was heartbroken that she was gone and angry that she worked herself so hard that it led to her death. I needed to say out loud, "Mom, I forgive you for leaving me." I knew she had done everything she could for us, and I had told her every day how much I loved and appreciated her. I know she wouldn't have chosen to leave, and I long for the day we will be reunited. Until then, I will live life fully, as she would have wanted.

A significant part of this journey was learning to ask for forgiveness for myself. In *Psalm 32:1-5* (NIV), the Bible emphasizes the importance of acknowledging sin and asking God for forgiveness. *Psalm 139:23-24* (NIV) states, "Search me, God, and know my heart; test me and know my anxious thoughts. See if there is any offensive way in me, and lead me in the way everlasting."

Ask God to reveal anything you need to forgive yourself for. When we ask, He reveals, but we must be willing and ready to accept what is shown.

Studying God's Word is an ongoing process. As the Bible says, people perish for lack of knowledge. We must remember that forgiveness does not mean keeping a tally of wrongs done to us. To forgive is to let go and let God.

There are those who have endured unimaginable acts. These experiences may require therapy and deep healing. Start today. It is no coincidence that you are reading this book. Remember the parable of the man, the flood, the helicopter, and the Coast Guard? Perhaps this book is your rescue.

Forgiveness is not saying, "What you did was okay." It acknowledges that something happened that caused pain and that it wasn't right. Forgiveness is choosing not to let that pain turn into bitterness that can consume you. Bitterness can become a silent poison, eroding joy and peace. Forgiveness is the antidote that restores your heart and mind. Unresolved pain can manifest as physical and emotional illnesses. But when you forgive, that weight is lifted from your shoulders and your heart.

During my journey, I learned to write down moments where I felt resentment or animosity and journal about my forgiveness. It does not always require a conversation with the other person. Forgiveness is growth and empowerment. It can be a letter you write but never send, or a conversation with God acknowledging the pain and releasing it. I invite you to try this: write down who or what you need to forgive, and why. Reflect on how carrying that burden has affected you and imagine what it would feel like to let it go.

You have the power to forgive on your terms. Only you know your situation, so be discerning. If direct confrontation puts you in danger, then it's best avoided. Your peace and safety are most important.

Remember, forgiveness is an act of strength, not weakness. It's a witness to your resilience and trust in God's promises. Let me take a moment to pray for you:

Dear Heavenly Father,

I come before You today to intercede for Your child reading this passage. Father, thank You for all You have done, for what You are doing now, and for what You will continue to do.

Thank You for clearing obstacles from their path and for winning unseen battles on their behalf. Father, I pray for continued healing and supernatural faith.

Reveal any areas in their life that require forgiveness and repentance. Remove the scales from their eyes so they can see and accept what You reveal. May they feel Your comforting presence, as they open their heart to forgiveness, knowing they are never alone in this journey. Touch their heart and help them forgive those who have hurt them, knowing that forgiveness will set them free. Heal their wounds and make them whole.

I pray for their peace and that today marks the start of a new life. I pray that they give You their full 'yes.'

In Jesus name, I pray. Amen.

Chapter 17: Be Still

Be still, and know that I am God; I will be exalted among the nations, I will be exalted in the earth."

— Psalm 46:10 (NIV)

* * *

When you decide to give God your *yes*, life may not change overnight. There is still work to be done. Being still in the Lord is a vital part of this journey. You might wonder, what does that mean, and how does it look in practice? In today's fast-paced world, where people are constantly rushing from one task to another—microwave meals, fast food, and busy schedules—being still can feel unnatural.

Being still in the Lord means being intentional about dedicating time to God. I mentioned earlier the importance of intentionality with your time. Being still means allowing your mind to be free from distractions so that you can hear God's voice. Having a schedule is fine, but ensure that God is at the forefront. Ask Him if everything on your schedule aligns with His will. If it doesn't, be willing to change it. Prioritizing God should be the first order of business when planning your day. When I made God the centerpiece of my day, I found myself approaching challenges with newfound strength and clarity. Tasks that once overwhelmed me seemed manageable, as if God was subtly guiding my steps.

God works for our good and desires what is best for us, but we must also be willing to do our part. Sit in His presence. When you wake up, thank God and praise Him before doing anything else. Lie there and talk to Him. Share your plans for the day. I often talk to God silently, thanking Him for allowing me to wake up with a sound mind, the ability to move, take care of myself, and worship Him. We often take these simple gifts for granted.

Have a meaningful conversation with God without asking for anything. Just sit and talk—share your thoughts, your relationships, your day at work. Avoid asking for things or complaining during this time. This time is meant to shift the focus from what you need to who God is, fostering a relationship rooted in love and trust rather than constant requests. Imagine if you were a parent and your child came to you daily, only to complain or ask for something—you'd become frustrated.

As parents, we often cherish when our children simply come to us to share good news or talk. There will always be a time to seek help and express grievances, but use this moment to create a deeper spiritual connection with your Heavenly Father.

Ask God how He feels about your outfit or your hairstyle. Talk to Him throughout the day. Learn to seek His guidance before making significant decisions, and wait for His response. Remember, God has given us the ability to discern situations, but we must limit distractions to hear Him clearly. Sometimes, His answers come in whispers or through unexpected moments. Trust that even silence has meaning and purpose in your journey. Often, we forget that our timing is not the same as God's timing.

Create a schedule today, designating a specific place and time to speak with God. Don't just fit Him into your day; build your day around Him. Give Him your complete, undivided attention. By minimizing distractions and focusing on God, you are declaring, "God, you are a priority in my life, and I value our relationship." Know that each moment you spend in stillness with God strengthens your bond with Him, nurturing a peace that will carry you through life's storms.

I have learned to be still in the Lord. I asked Him to help me understand His Word so that I could live abundantly. He answered by sending incredible destiny helpers.

As I sit here reflecting on all that has been said and done, I remember God telling me that He has known me since I was a little girl —and I knew Him, too. Embracing stillness taught me that while life moves at a relentless pace, God's peace is found in the pauses. It's in those quiet moments that His voice is clearest and His love most evident.

As you take steps to be still, remember that God's voice is often found not in the noise, but in the quiet whispers of your heart. Be still and know that He is with you, guiding and loving you every step of the way.

Father,

Thank You for being my friend, my provider, my protector, and my father.

Love Always,
Your Daughter Natasha

Closing Prayer

Dear Heavenly Father,

I thank You for Your grace and mercy. I thank You for allowing me to share my testimonies with the world. As I step out of the old and into the new, I embrace being Your child. I can stand firmly and take my rightful place as Your daughter. Father, I pray that You touch every person reading this book. I pray that You touch the people who are in their lives. I pray that You provide light to their feet and direction for their hearts. Enter into their lives and make the old new for them.

Father, I shout Your praises and thank You for Your unconditional love. I ask that You please provide a blanket over our nation, a blanket over the people who are reading this book. I pray for a blanket of protection and peace. I pray for their minds and souls. Father, soften their hearts, lift the scales from their eyes, and uncover their ears so they can hear and see You. I pray they have everlasting life in You. Father, the love I have for You cannot even be explained. I thank You, Father, for allowing this book to come to completion, and I pray this book is the light to someone's feet so that they can see the path to You. Make no mistake, it is not by coincidence that You have read this book.

Closing Prayer

I pray my testimony reveals that there is light at the end of the tunnel no matter what you're going through, no matter how bad the storm. Even if you feel like you have nothing left and no more to give, I am here to let you know your breakthrough is near. Please do not give up, do not turn your back on God, and do not give up on Him. You may feel like God has left you, but He hasn't. Hold on!

Father, right now, in the name of Jesus, I pray that You touch this person and heal their heart. I pray today for a supernatural breakthrough for the person reading this book. Hold them while they sleep tonight; hold Your sons and daughters in Your arms. I pray that every person who reads this book is healed.

In Jesus' mighty name. Amen

Acknowledgments

With a heart full of gratitude, I want to first thank my Almighty Heavenly Father for loving me unconditionally. Thank You, Father, for allowing me to share my testimony and glorify Your name. Thank You for Your grace and mercy, which have guided me through every step of my journey.

I am deeply grateful for my supportive family and friends who stood by me, listening and encouraging me through all of life's ups and downs. Your unwavering love and support have been a cornerstone in my life.

I also wish to express my heartfelt thanks to my work family. Your kindness, support, and shared moments of joy have helped me navigate some of the most challenging times in my life. The prayers, counsel, love, and unwavering encouragement you offered have been invaluable to me.

To the dedicated Prophetess and Apostle who faithfully obeyed God's word and carried out His mission and message, thank you. I am also deeply thankful to the Pastors who honorably preached the word of God, guiding me with wisdom and truth. To the Grief Recovery Program and Pastor Peggy Norton, thank you for the vital support and guidance you provided. A special thank you to the Prophetess for leading the 25-day fast that helped break generational curses and covenants.

I pray that my mother is reading this from heaven, smiling down on me with joy. Thank You, Father, for blessing me with a mother who loved me unconditionally—my earth angel, now my heavenly angel. God, You not only sent me one angel, but You also blessed me with another.

To my daughter, Anaya: thank you for loving me unconditionally. When I think of you, I am reminded of God's profound love for me, as He sent me you. We have faced so much together and emerged stronger each time. Because we had each other, every challenge felt like a walk in the park. I love you beyond words, and I am incredibly proud of everything you have achieved and all that you will continue to accomplish. No matter what path you choose in life, I will always have your back.

About the Author

Natasha Janise is an educator, writer, and lifelong learner with a passion for transforming life's moments into meaningful stories. Inspired by her childhood traditions and the beauty of the world around her, she began writing as a way to capture and share the joy and challenges of life.

With over 20 years of experience in special education, Natasha holds five advanced degrees and has mentored countless teachers while dedicating her career to empowering others. Her writing explores themes of faith, resilience, and hope, encouraging readers to trust God through life's storms and embrace their unique gifts.

When she's not writing, Natasha enjoys spa days, walking, and indulging in her favorite pastime—singing (enthusiastically, if not always on key). She cherishes quiet moments of reflection, family gatherings, and diving into research, especially on topics related to health and wellness.

To get in touch with Natasha Janise:

IG: @NatashaJaniseAuthor
Email: NatashaJaniseAuthor@gmail.com

www.ingramcontent.com/pod-product-compliance
Lightning Source LLC
Chambersburg PA
CBHW051538120626
46551CB00013B/1284